D1580484

Maths on the Go

Also by Rob Eastaway and Mike Askew

Maths for Mums and Dads

More Maths for Mums and Dads

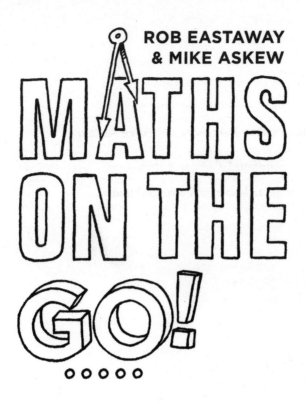

ROB EASTAWAY
& MIKE ASKEW

MATHS
ON THE
GO!

ooooo

101 FUN WAYS
TO PLAY
WITH MATHS

◼ SQUARE PEG

Published by Square Peg 2016

2 4 6 8 10 9 7 5 3 1

First published in Great Britain in 2016 by
Square Peg,
Vintage Books,
20 Vauxhall Bridge Road,
London SW1V 2SA

www.vintage-books.co.uk

A Penguin Random House Company

Penguin
Random House
UK

www. Penguinrandomhouse.com

A CIP catalogue record for this book
is available from the British Library

ISBN 9780224101622

Printed and bound in Great Britain by Clays Ltd, St Ives PLC

Contents

Investigation and Discovery

Quick Games to Play Anywhere

Maths at Home

Mealtimes

Doing the Shopping

On a Journey

End of the Day

Games with Simple Props

Out and About

Maths Magic

How to Use This Book

This is a book full of games, activities and ideas for how to play with maths, to engage your child in mathematical thinking as part of your and their everyday lives. The ideas have been loosely grouped into themes to help you find useful ones quickly, though as you'll see there are many that work just as well in the car as at the dinner table. To speed things further, there is an index at the back so you can look up ideas by maths topic (how can I help my child with times tables?).

Most of the ideas work best with children aged five to eleven. Beyond eleven hormones start to kick in, and even if you already have a strong track record of 'playing' maths with your child, you're going to meet increasing resistance as they enter secondary school, and the way you do it will have to be correspondingly subtle and sophisticated.

Five to eleven is a wide range. Obviously, most eleven year-olds will find routine counting games a little beneath them, and five year-olds will be baffled by challenges involving times tables, but many activities can be adapted to the age and aptitude of your child. Each activity has a key to indicate the age range for which it is likely to work best, but this is no more than a guideline. (See the key on page xv.)

As a rule, the younger the child the more enthusiastic and accepting they are. An announcement like 'Hey, let's see if we can find an odd number!' generally works with five year-olds, and not with someone twice their age ('Give it a rest, Mum.').

One of the best ways we've found of engaging children older than ten is when they have a younger sibling or relative. It's often possible to try one of the maths ideas in the book on the younger child, but making sure that the older one is listening in (this is particularly effective when sitting around the table for a meal). The older child, while pretending to be too cool for this stuff, will quietly be taking it all in, and will often end up joining in – it's a chance for them to demonstrate their superior knowledge.

There are more ideas here than you are ever likely to use – some will fit your style more than others. Play to your strengths, and to your child's interests. Obsessed with football? Sport is great for mental arithmetic (What's the Score? page 89). Minecraft addicts? Get them to calculate their screen time (page 87). But do be prepared to try ideas out even if they don't immediately grab your interest. Although it's ideal to have maths activities that you and your child both enjoy, you might be surprised to find your child having fun with things that don't appeal to you, and their enjoyment might even be contagious.

Everything we've suggested here is meant to be entertaining, and should be done with a smile.

But however much fun you have, we would strongly encourage you not to overdo it. Some parents manage to seamlessly squeeze in a mathematical idea every time they go on an outing, but your child may well spot you attempting to crowbar in some maths when they aren't in the mood, and the last thing you want is for them to start resisting.

Some of the ideas we've suggested tend to work better when you don't make them all about maths. The more that children experience maths as a natural part of everyday life, the less likely it is that, as teenagers, they will ask that heart-sinking question: 'When am I ever going to need this?'

Getting Started – a few basics

Before launching into doing maths, it can help to have a few items in place that make it much easier to be spontaneous. There aren't many things in our list, and you probably have most of them to hand already, but it makes a big difference always keeping a pack of playing cards (for example) in a convenient drawer, rather than having to search around the house to find one. The following are useful:

Paper and a pencil

Scissors and sticky tape

Playing cards

An analogue clock

A digital clock

Dice

An egg timer

A tape measure

A jar of dried beans or other countable items

A calculator (your phone probably has one on it)

Age Key

As a guide, we've provided a key for each activity suggesting which ages it is best suited to. Some activities can work (with a bit of adapting) for everyone, but others are much more age specific, for example because they are based on more sophisticated maths knowledge.

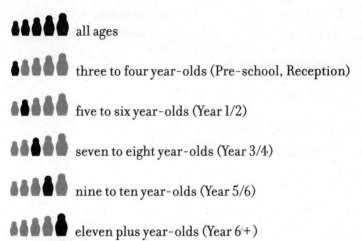

🪆🪆🪆🪆🪆 all ages

🪆🪆🪆🪆🪆 three to four year-olds (Pre-school, Reception)

🪆🪆🪆🪆🪆 five to six year-olds (Year 1/2)

🪆🪆🪆🪆🪆 seven to eight year-olds (Year 3/4)

🪆🪆🪆🪆🪆 nine to ten year-olds (Year 5/6)

🪆🪆🪆🪆🪆 eleven plus year-olds (Year 6+)

So: 🪆🪆🪆🪆🪆 means this activity is best suited to seven to ten year-olds.

How to Talk Maths

Talking maths with your children can feel a bit forced so here are some tips to help you incorporate maths ideas into everyday conversation without making it sound like a lesson. The secret is to keep discussions about maths as light and playful as possible.

Playing Dumb

Give your child a chance to answer before you do

Helps with: Building your child's confidence, particularly when doing money calculations.

When you've posed a maths question – for example, 'If this cost eighty-four pence, how much change will there be from a pound?' – the silence that follows can be painful. It can be tempting either to hurry your child along ('Come on, what do you have to add to eighty-four to make a hundred?') or to answer the question yourself. The trouble is that this knocks your child's confidence, so try to resist the temptation always to be the expert who knows the right answer. It can be much more effective to treat a calculation as a collaboration, something you and your child are doing together, rather than a test.

One tactic is to play dumb: to attempt the question you want answered yourself, but get stuck. Start going through your thinking, but then make an error and correct yourself. 'Let's see, eighty-four from ninety is five – is that right? – eighty-four plus five is . . . no, that's eighty-nine.' This is inviting your child to help you.

If they come up with an answer before you do, and they get it wrong, start by accepting the answer. 'Oh, yes, a hundred take away eighty-four is fourteen. That's right, eighty-four add fourteen is a hundred...Wait a minute, is that right...?'

(All of this can be done mentally, but most children find it helpful to see calculations written down. This is where a graffiti wall can come in very handy – see page 75.)

Oh yes, 100 take away 84 is 14.
That's right, 84 add 14 is 100...
Wait a minute, is that right?

Saying 'Yet'

The best response to the phrase 'I can't' is the word 'Yet'

Helps with: Building confidence in solving maths problems, realising that finding maths hard is OK.

Sometime in your child's maths career – possibly very early on – they are going to encounter some maths that is hard. Maybe it will be doing short division, or working out how to add fractions. What it leads to is the complaint, 'I can't do it!' And the simple response to that is the word 'yet'. You can't add fractions *yet*, you don't get all your divisions right *yet*. That simple word encourages what teachers like to call a 'growth mindset', in other words maths is something you get better at with practice, rather than something you can either do or not do. A bit like playing the piano.

This tip comes in most handy at homework time, but it applies anywhere and to anything that your child is struggling with – not just maths.

3

Think Aloud

When doing calculations, think aloud

Helps with: Understanding that answers don't appear by magic, but need to be worked out – and also that there's more than one way of getting to the right answer.

If your child is with you when you are working out the answer to something, make a point of doing it out loud. If you happen to be very good at mental calculations, slow down a bit so they can follow what you are doing. This will send a very positive message that you need to work at getting to a solution – and also that there can be several different ways of doing so.

By calculating aloud you are also being a good role model – your child will feel it's normal to do the same. It's especially good if you occasionally make mistakes, so that they can see that mistakes are normal and nothing to be ashamed of (though you do want the right answer in the end, of course).

Teach Me

Get your child to teach you how to do maths

Helps with: Your child's confidence and also helps you to understand the maths they are being taught.

Get your child to teach you some of the maths they have recently been taught in school, even if you think you know what they've done. If, for instance, they come home and say they have been doing take-aways, ask them to give you an example of the sort of sum and to explain how they do it.

It's very likely that the methods you learned at school were different from the ones your child is learning. You'll be itching to demonstrate your method, but try to bite your

tongue – there is a danger that you will only confuse them. If you do want to demonstrate your own method, try it on a different occasion. One method at a time is our advice.

If their explanation starts to go wrong, resist the temptation to 'fix' it – allow them to carry on explaining. This often results in them sorting out the bug in the explanation for themselves. But even if that doesn't happen, it's better simply to acknowledge that something is not quite right and invite them to see if they can sort things out and explain it to you tomorrow.

You've Worked Hard!

Praise effort rather than success

Helps with: Encouraging your child to keep trying.

When your child does well in a maths test, it's oh, so tempting to tell them how clever they are. 'Well done, you're a bit of a genius.' The trouble is, all the psychological evidence suggests that this is absolutely the wrong thing to do. Carol Dweck, an American educational psychologist, published a world-famous study which showed that children who are told they are brilliant at maths tend to become more anxious and to perform worse when the maths gets harder. If they were 'clever' when they got the answers right, then when they start to struggle they think that maybe this is a sign of their cleverness disappearing – and there's nothing they can do about it.

The thing to praise, Dweck confirmed, is effort. 'Well done, you've worked hard on those problems.' Praising and rewarding effort means children feel good about working hard, even if the results aren't great. They are more likely to try hard next time. And while natural ability clearly does have some bearing on maths ability, what really makes children better at maths is doing lots of practice. So the more they are encouraged to work hard, the better they'll get.

Big Ego Arnold

Use your hand to make a puppet with an inflated maths ego

Helps with: Solving maths questions without it feeling like a test.

In the tip on Playing Dumb (page 3), we mentioned how it helps if, instead of testing your child, maths is something you do with them as a collaboration. And there's one thing that can really help to get your child on your side, and that's to create a common enemy. This is where puppets come in.

Raise your right hand and form the fingers and thumb to make a mouth. That's it: you now have a puppet, and it's ready to enter the conversation. 'Hello, my name is Arnold,' says the hand, 'and I'm brilliant at maths. I know what three times eight is, and nobody else does – I bet you don't know what it is.'

It's hard to resist a taunt like that, and most children are very keen to prove Arnold wrong. 'It's twenty-four!' Arnold gets increasingly frustrated as he discovers that he isn't quite the unique maths genius that he thought he was.

If your child isn't sure about the answer, you can send Arnold away. 'OK, I'll pop away for a moment, but when I come back I'm sure you won't know the answer,' says your hand before it marches off under the table. Now you and your child can

work out the answer together. Incredibly (and charmingly) children as old as six or seven are perfectly happy treating you and your hand as completely different people, so when you've come up with the answer and Arnold the hand puppet returns, your child will happily boast that they have the answer, and delight in how annoyed Arnold is.

7

Naughty Puppet

Frampton is a mean puppet who loves spoiling patterns

Helps with: Practising calculation and pattern spotting.

Like Arnold (page 10), Frampton is a hand puppet. But he's a mean one. Nothing gives him more pleasure than spoiling patterns, counting wrongly and getting sums wrong. 'I know how to count to ten: one, four, three, six, eight...' or 'I know how to count in threes...three, six, ten, thirteen.'

Frampton also takes pleasure in keeping secrets, by deliberately hiding numbers. 'I know what seven plus eight is and I've hidden the answer where nobody will find it,' he says, ideally followed by a mean pantomime cackle: 'Bru-ha-ha-ha.'

Children love nothing more than defeating a villain like Frampton by announcing that the number he has hidden is fifteen. 'Doh, how did you know that?'

Scoring Points

Create an incentive to try challenges through the day

Helps with: Any maths (or other) activity you want to encourage.

Announce that today there's going to be a challenge to get as many points as possible. Or to get to ten points by a deadline like lunchtime. You can be vague about what the winner will actually receive; you may not even know what the prize is yet and you can just leave it as a surprise. At those moments in the day when you want to encourage or discourage certain behaviour or activities, you announce, 'OK, there are two points available for this.'

What this does is give a context in which you can set any tasks or pose any challenges you like, anywhere. And that can include maths questions. On the way to school, you can say, 'OK, one point if you can correctly tell me how many centimetres there are in a metre.' Or, 'One point for working out the change when I buy this litre of milk.'

If there's more than one child involved in the game, make sure it's fair, while also keeping the scores reasonably close.

Scoring points becomes an end in itself, and if it's presented as fun and exciting and done with a smile, then anything from practising times tables to taking another three spoonfuls of this 'disgusting' soup can be worth doing.

Maths to Talk About

Here are ideas that you can introduce in those odd
moments when there's a chance for you and your child to
have a conversation – on the way to school, when you're
eating together, waiting in a queue, even at bedtime.

Spot the Deliberate Mistake

Sneak nonsense into a story to keep children on their mathematical toes

Helps with: Any calculations or maths understanding.

This works a bit like the BBC radio show *The Unbelievable Truth* in which a guest attempts to sneak several facts into a set of 'lies'. In this game, however, your child's job will be to shout 'Bzzz!' every time you say something that is *wrong*. If they buzz correctly they get a point, and if they buzz incorrectly they lose one.

You could make this purely maths facts: 'Eight plus three equals eleven, four times four is fifteen...' 'BZZZ!' But it's more fun, and more repeatable, if you intersperse maths facts with other knowledge. For example, you could tell a tale about Henry VIII:

'One day, Henry the Eighth decided he needed to work out how much he owned. "I will need to use my calculator," he said...'

'BZZZ! They didn't have calculators in those days!' (One point.)

'"Let's see," said Henry, "I have five castles in Wales and twenty-three castles in England, so that makes twenty-nine castles altogether..."'

'BZZZ! It's twenty-eight castles, not twenty-nine.' (Another point.)

You can make up all sorts of amusing anecdotes about how Henry switched on the TV, went to the doctor to get some tablets for his headache, undid his tie because he was getting hot. But you should put some true statements in as well: 'Altogether he had six wives, who, between them, had sixty toes.'

One-Word Parrot

Help your parrot to look like a maths whizz

Helps with: Building up difficult calculations.

Try this round the table at mealtimes or out and about in a restaurant when you're waiting for the food to arrive. Introduce Priscilla the amazing calculating parrot (as ever, Priscilla can be your hand).

Ask Priscilla a maths question and she will give you the answer. 'Priscilla, what is three plus four?' 'Seven,' squawks the parrot.

Remarkable. This parrot is clearly a mathematician. Maybe she could take her act to the circus.

'Priscilla, what is ten take away five?' 'Seven.'

Oh dear. Try again. 'Priscilla, what is two times six?' 'Seven.' Oh no, it looks as though whatever Priscilla is asked, her

Pi equals 3.141592653589793238462643............

only response is to say seven. In that case, to make her look like a genius parrot, we'd better find questions to which the answer is seven. Now it becomes a challenge to think of more and more convoluted questions that end up at seven. 'What's sixteen divided by four, plus three?' 'What is three squared, plus five, divided by two?' Making up difficult maths questions becomes a fun game.

How Long Until…?

Deliberately misunderstand 'How long?' questions

Helps with: Understanding proportions and the scales of things.

'How long until Mummy's home?' 'How long until my birthday?' 'How long till we get there?' These questions are all about time, and time is a very hard thing to picture. So when your child asks you one of these questions, instead of stating the number of hours or weeks or months, hold your hands apart and say, 'About this much.' They'll be confused. How can an amount of time be the space between your hands?

But you can then show them by comparing your answer to something else they know.

'So far on our journey we've taken this long –' show with your hands – 'and the amount we still have to go is this long –' change the distance between your hands. Immediately they can see that the amount of time they have to wait might be the same, or twice as long, or a fraction as long, as a time they already know about.

You can do this in lots of different ways. 'This is how long it is until tomorrow,' you say, showing a tiny gap between your fingers. 'And this is how long it is until your birthday –' as you march to the window, stretching your arms out to show how much further that is.

12

Age Fractions

Help your child work out exactly how old they are

Helps with: Fractions.

From a very early age children are fascinated by their age, and by how long it will be until their next birthday. So they quickly grasp the idea that there are numbers like 'half' and 'quarter' between their last birthday and the next.

What's mathematically neat about the calendar is that twelve months can be divided into lots of different fractions: six months is half, four months is one third, three months is a quarter, two months is one sixth. (The fact that twelve can be divided in so many ways is one reason why it was chosen as the number of months in the first place.)

So when your child is five years and five months, let them know they are *nearly* five and a half. By the time they are six, they should be able to grasp that six months is half a year, and three months quarter of a year (you can draw a diagram) so you can begin to help them work out for themselves what age fraction they are.

You can even pose age puzzles. 'You are eight and two sixths and your friend is eight and a half – which of you is older?'

When Will You be Able to Buy Wayne Rooney?

Kids have little idea how big a million is

Helps with: Estimation, and getting a sense of the magnitude of different numbers.

This can be used at any time, but it's particularly interesting and fun when your child receives some pocket money or a birthday present of money.

If your child has just received £10 from Aunt Flora, ask yourself aloud, 'I wonder how long it will be before you can buy Wayne Rooney with all this money that you are saving?' (Of course, for Wayne Rooney, substitute any really expensive object living or dead that your child takes a particular interest in – the crown jewels, an Aston Martin etc.) Open up discussion about how much Wayne Rooney costs, and then begin to guess how long it really will take to save up enough money. 'If you keep getting ten pounds from Aunt Flora every birthday, do you think you'll be able to buy him when you're twenty-one? What about when you're eighty? I wonder if Wayne Rooney will still be alive then ... OK, what if we ask Aunt Flora to start giving you ten pounds every week?'

Needless to say, most children massively underestimate how many £10 notes it takes to buy anything expensive. In the case of a footballer who's on a salary of, say, £5 million per year, it would take 10,000 years of putting £10 into the piggy bank before you had enough to even pay for one year's salary!

Plan That Party

Children have a vested interest in planning their birthday party

Helps with: Arithmetical skills, shapes.

Are you fed up of planning your child's party every year? Why should you do all the work? It's their party after all!

As they get older you can start to involve them in some of the planning – and if there's one project of particular interest to your child, it's their own party.

Here are a few ideas for how they can help:

- Setting the number of friends to invite, and counting to check they are inside the limit.

- Decorating the cake, making sure that the sweets on the top are evenly spaced. How many Smarties are needed around the perimeter? Slightly more than three times as many as along the diameter?

- Party bags. Tell them the budget for party bags, and they can work out what they can afford to put in each one. (You get final veto, of course.)

- Budgeting. Give them a menu from their favourite restaurant and an overall budget to take a group of friends there. How many friends can they invite?

15

Dog Years

Work out your age in dog, cat and hamster years

Helps with: Multiplying and dividing by seven (and other numbers).

Everyone knows that to work out a dog's age in human years, you just multiply it by seven. Likewise cat years are about six human years, while hamster years are about thirty-five. That used to be the rule, anyway. These days pet experts like to be more sophisticated. After all, dogs can start having puppies in their first year, and how many seven-year-old people can do that?

So, depending on how complicated you want to make it, you can do any of the following:

- Work out the age of your pet in human years (multiply by seven for dogs, by six for cats, ten for some gold-fish, and thirty-five for hamsters).

- Work out your ages if you were a dog, cat, goldfish or hamster (which means dividing by those numbers).

- Use the sophisticated rules for all of the above. In the case of dogs, it's something like this:

  - First dog year = twelve human years
  - Second dog year = twelve human years
  - All later dog years = four human years

So if your dog is five, that converts to twenty-four (for its first two years) plus $4 \times 3 = 12$ for the next three years, which makes thirty-six years. Or, if you want the formula:

$$\text{Human age} = 4 \times \text{dog age} + 16$$
(as long as the dog is at least two years old)

You can rearrange that to get:

$$\text{Dog age} = (\text{human age} - 16) \div 4.$$

Yes, your kids might even be up for investigating some simple algebra when pets are involved.

16

Would You Rather…?

Which of these would make you richest?

You will need: A calculator.

Helps with: Estimating and calculating.

Set your child a mathematical choice challenge, such as:

> Would you rather have your height as a
> stack of £1 coins
>
> *or*
>
> your weight in 20p coins?

> Would you rather have a penny for every day
> you have been alive
>
> *or*
>
> a penny for every millimetre tall you are?

Chat about how the choice could be investigated and set your child off to work out which they think might be the better deal.

Encourage them to make up similar challenges of their own.

17

Break Those Biscuits

Sharing becomes much more interesting when there's a remainder

Helps with: Division and fractions.

Suppose there are three of you and there are five biscuits left. What do you do? Your child has a vested interest in this, so there's lots of potential for 'doing the maths'. And if possible, you also want your child to do the maths. If they are stumped, do some thinking aloud. What if we have two biscuits each? Drat, there aren't enough, so that isn't fair! One each? That's good, but what about the two that are left over?

Children come up with all sorts of solutions. Maybe break the spare biscuits in half, so all three get half a biscuit extra. That still leaves a spare half, which you can split into three pieces (in this case you could point out that one third of a half is one sixth), so you all end up with one whole biscuit plus half a biscuit plus a sixth. Which is the same as one and four sixths. Which is the same as one and two thirds.

One of us witnessed three children in the back of a car, aged eleven, eight and five, who had four sweets left. Their parents were in the front. All three children got involved in working out a solution, which ranged from having one each and splitting the last one between their parents to having one each and playing a game to see who should get the last one. In the end, they opted for equal shares, so each took it in turns to attempt to bite off one third of the final sweet for themselves. Needless to say the third child ended up with a gooey mash, though as compensation it did seem to be the biggest bit.

Zequals

Doing big, rough calculations in your head

Helps with: Estimation, mental arithmetic.

Imagine being able to work out a calculation like 365 × 24 in your head. As it happens, almost anybody can – as long as you're happy with the answer being only roughly right.

Zequals is a fun way of ruthlessly rounding numbers so that every number you deal with becomes simple. Using Zequals, whenever you encounter a number, you immediately round it to a single digit followed by zeroes (if it's bigger than ten). So for example:

> 18 zequals 20.
>
> 142 zequals 100.
>
> 2.3 zequals 2.
>
> 1,948,103 zequals 2 million.

This is known as rounding a number to 'one significant figure' – which means the same as rounding to the nearest unit, ten, hundred and so on. The only thing that tends to catch people out is that Zequals doesn't do anything to the numbers one to nine (they are already rounded to the nearest unit, so three zequals three).

Children as young as seven or eight can master Zequals, and once they have done so, they can do difficult calculations in their heads. Which means you can use Zequals to do calculations without the need of a calculator, just for the fun of it. How many hours are there in a year? That's 365 days × 24 hours. 365 zequals 400, and 24 zequals 20, so the answer is 400 × 20 = 8,000. (The exact answer is 8,760, but a typical eight-year-old would take minutes to work that out using pencil and paper.)

Investigation and Discovery

Here are ideas you can give to your child that might set them off investigating. And there's nothing better than your child keeping themselves occupied!

Fractional Relatives

What proportion of you is Scottish?

Helps with: Fractions that add up to one, pie charts and percentages.

Most of us have an interesting ancestor or relative or two who comes from another country, be that Ireland, Poland or Nigeria. Children who discover their parents came from different places like the idea of calling themselves 'half Italian and half English', or even 'half Yorkshire and half Devon'.

But you can take this further. If your mother was English but your father came from, say, Australia, where did their parents come from? Maybe (to take one of the authors as an example) one paternal grandparent was born in Australia but the other was born in Scotland. In which case you'd be half English, one quarter Australian and one quarter Scottish.

This can keep going further back through the generations – maybe (to take the same author as an example) you're really five eighths English, one eighth Australian and one quarter Scottish.

You can use a tree diagram to map out ancestors; each time you go back a generation the fraction gets halved. And whatever your ancestral fractions are, the total must always add up to one!

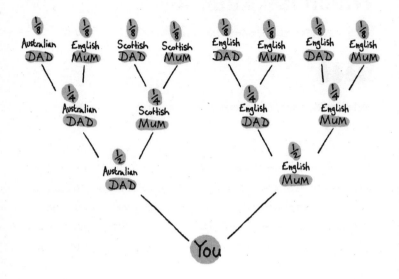

Which is More?

Discovering that the order of multiplying doesn't matter

Helps with: Multiplication.

Which would you prefer, eight bags with four sweets in them, or four bags with eight sweets in them? If your child is young, they probably think that one of the options gives them more sweets – though they are split over which one it is. The easiest way to check is by counting. With four rows of eight Smarties, they can see that four lots of eight must be the same as eight lots of four.

Older children will know that four eights and eight fours are the same (that's one of the ways of simplifying times tables – you don't need to learn eight times four if you already know four times eight). But they might still be confused if you push the numbers beyond ten. Which is more, 486 boxes with 23 sweets in, or 23 boxes with 486 sweets in? How can they be sure?

Knowing that the order of multiplication makes no difference to the answer is an important fact that comes back time and again in maths, so it's great to reinforce it when you can.

'Have a guess what $1 \times 2 \times 3 \times 4 \times 5 \times 6 \times 7 \times 8 \times 9$ is. Now have a guess what $9 \times 8 \times 7 \times 6 \times 5 \times 4 \times 3 \times 2 \times 1$ is.' Even adults tend to think that the second answer is bigger than the first – but a calculator will confirm that the two are the same.

21

I've Heard That...

Investigate whether bizarre 'facts' are true

Helps with: Estimation and rough calculations.

This is a good game for mealtimes, or other times when there is a bit of waiting about and time to fill with conversation. Start by quoting some 'fact' that you've heard recently (maybe on the news), and use it to start an investigation. Or you could use one of these 'facts':

- 'I've heard that three times round your head is about the same as your height — let's get a piece of string and find out.'

- 'I've heard that most people are almost square; that their height is the same as their stretch (the distance from left to right fingertips with arms outstretched) — can I check?'

- 'I've heard that when you are twice as tall, you weigh eight times as much – that can't be right, can it?'

- 'I've heard that a grasshopper can jump a distance up to twenty times its length. How far could you jump if you were as good as a grasshopper?'

- 'I've heard that a shrew eats around three quarters of its weight in food in a day. How much would you need to eat if you ate as much as a shrew?'

22

Win a Fiver – By Drawing It!

A motivating way to learn about scale and measurement

▲▲▲▲▲

Helps with: Geometry and measurement.

Take out a £5 note – or, if you're feeling brave, a tenner. Tell your child they have a chance to win the fiver if they can draw a diagram of it that is the right size. Then put the note back in your pocket. They've got to be close – their drawing has to be within an agreed limit of the exact shape. Depending on how old they are, that limit could be as much as a couple of centimetres, or as little as a few millimetres.

When they've drawn the rectangle that represents the note, place the real note over their diagram. The chances

that they'll be anywhere close are extremely remote (their drawing will be too big or too small), but there will be real excitement and drama as you build up to the moment when you make the comparison.

You can do the same with a £1 coin or 2p piece.

Try it again a week later to see if your child has got better. This game can run and run, and if they do ever produce a diagram that's accurate enough to your specifications, they'll have earned their prize!

Mirror, Mirror, on the Wall

Mysteries with reflection

Helps with: Ideas about geometry.

Mirrors are a delightful source of mathematical curiosities. That's one reason why they featured in Lewis Carroll's second story about Alice, *Through the Looking-Glass*.

- Get a spoon and look at your reflection in the back of it: your face is all distorted, with a giant nose. But when you look at yourself in the front of the spoon... your face is suddenly upside down. Why?

- Find a mirror or reflecting glass (such as a shop window) where your child can see their face, but not their feet. Wonder out loud to yourself: 'How far would we have to go back before we could see our feet in this mirror?' A few feet? The other side of the road? The curious truth is that if the mirror is vertical and the ground is horizontal (as is the case with most

WHERE ARE MY FEET?!

windows and pavements, for example) then it doesn't matter how far back you stand, you'll never be able to see your feet.

- Here's a question that gets harder to answer the more you think about it. When you look at yourself in a mirror, your right hand becomes your left hand and vice versa. Why is it that mirrors switch things from left to right, and not from top to bottom?

How Much Are You Worth?

Turn words into numbers

Helps with: Addition and money.

There are twenty-six letters in the alphabet. Turn each letter into a number of pence, so A = 1p, B = 2p, C = 3p, all the way to Z = 26p.

Now work out the value of your name. For example, MIKE is 13 + 9 + 11 + 5 = 38p.

Who has the more expensive name? How much more?

It helps to have a name with letters that are late in the alphabet, so children who have Zs and Ys have a big advantage over the Bs and Cs, while the best vowels to have are U and O. Zoe is worth more than Abigail.

Find out who the most valuable person you know is. Is there anyone whose first name is worth exactly £1?

What is the longest name you could buy for exactly £1?

Guess How Many

Recreate the old funfair game of 'How Many in the Jar?'

You will need: A jar filled with some small dried items such as beans or macaroni.

Helps with: Number sense and appreciating large numbers.

This is a good activity to set up for your child to do while you are busy in the kitchen.

You and your child each guess how many beans, say, you think are in the jar.

You can first think together about how to check the number without counting all the items separately. For example:

- Count how many beans fill the lid of the jar or an egg cup, and then count how many times this could be filled.

- Spread a single layer of beans over the back of an envelope, and then see how many envelopes could be covered.

- Weigh out a scoop of beans and count how many it holds. How many scoops are there in the jar?

Then leave them to do the counting!

Paper Shapes

Make a kite and a pentagon from a scrap of paper

You will need: A piece of A4 paper.

Helps with: Geometry.

A humble scrap of A4 paper has a lot of maths curiosities in it. For a start, you can announce that you are about to make a kite. Here's how:

Fold the bottom-left corner up the right side:

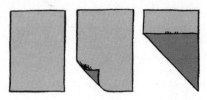

Then fold the top-left corner down to join the folded piece, like this:

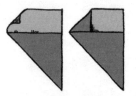

Now turn over the paper, and if you've done it accurately the shape is a perfectly symmetrical kite.

This only works with A4 paper, by the way. It's to do with the ratio of the lengths of the two sides of an A4 sheet of paper. The length of the long side (297mm) divided by the length of the short side (210mm) is 1.414, which is almost exactly the square root of 2. In other words 1.414 × 1.414 = 2 (or it does very nearly).

There's another nice shape you can make from your piece of paper. You'll need to carefully tear off a strip about two centimetres wide. Now tie the strip in a simple knot. When the knot is fairly tight, gently flatten it. A pentagon will emerge. You can see it more clearly if you tear off the two strips sticking out to the side.

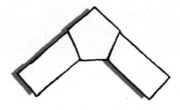

Just a Minute

Exactly how long is a minute?

You will need: A watch with a second hand or the timer on your phone.

Helps with: Counting, measuring time.

Take it in turns to estimate how long a minute lasts.

One of you has the timer and says 'Go'.

The other says 'Stop' when they think a minute is up.

How good are each of you at estimating how long a minute is?

Do you get better with practice?

(There's an old guide that says ten seconds lasts about as long as it takes to say, 'One ELEPHANT two ELEPHANT three ELEPHANT...' all the way to ten ELEPHANT. Does that improve your performance? Try it out. It does depend on how quickly you say 'ELEPHANT'.)

28

How Many Ways?

Counting different combinations can be a laugh

Helps with: Counting and combinations.

Your child's morning routine is probably fairly predictable. Maybe it's like this:

1 Wake up

2 Get out of bed

3 Have a wee

4 Take off pyjamas

5 Get dressed

6 Eat breakfast

7 Grab bag

8 Leave for school

So why not have some fun suggesting how they could mix it up. What if the first thing was 'Leave for school'? Would that work? What's the silliest order you can come up with? How about:

1 Grab bag

2 Get dressed

3 Leave for school

4 Have a wee

5 Eat Breakfast

6 Take off pyjamas

7 Get out of bed

8 Wake up

How many different combinations are there? (The answer is big. There are eight things you can do at the start, seven things left that can go second and so on. In fact, the total number of possible combinations is $8 \times 7 \times 6 \times 5 \times 4 \times 3 \times 2 \times 1$, which is 40,320. But how many of them would actually work?)

29

Handful of Coins

Which prices can you pay exactly?

Helps with: Money and calculating.

Pull out from your purse or pocket a handful of coins.

The challenge is to work out how much you could pay exactly, using some or all of these coins.

For example, suppose the coins you pull out are a 20p, a 10p, three 5p's, and a 2p.

Could you pay exactly 32p? Yes, 20p, 10p and 2p. What about 43p? No, the nearest you can get is 42p (20p, 10p, 5p, 5p, 2p).

This lends itself to puzzles that you can make up on the spur of the moment. For example, what is the most money you could have in 1p, 2p, 5p, 10p, 20p and 50p coins and not be able to pay exactly £1? You can have as many of each coin as you want.

Answer: It's possible to have £1.43 and still not be able to pay exactly £1. The coins have to be: one 50p, four 20p's, one 5p and four 2p's. Check it out!

Quick Games to Play Anywhere

There are often moments when your child could do with some distraction: standing in a queue, waiting at the doctor's surgery, or on a trip to the shops, for example. Here are some quick games to have up your sleeve for such occasions. They require no props and, in many cases, need only take a minute or so.

30

Rock, Paper...Add!

An instant adding or multiplying game played with fingers

Helps with: Arithmetical skills.

This game is played a little like 'Rock, Paper, Scissors'. Two or three can play and each person starts with one hand behind their back. Take it in turns to chant 'one, two, show'. On the word 'show', everyone brings forward their hand, holding up between five fingers and none. The first person to correctly call out the total number of fingers scores a point.

As your child gets better at this, you could hide both hands and show a number to ten. And if there are just two of you, you could call out the answer to both numbers of fingers multiplied together. To test the harder times-table multiplications you can make it a rule that each player has to hold out at least five fingers.

31

Twenty

A counting game that works for all ages

Helps with: Counting, spotting patterns and finding rules.

This counting game works as well with a five year-old as with a sixty year-old. The rules are simple: take it in turns counting up from one to twenty, and the aim is to get your opponent to say 'Twenty'. When it's your turn you can count one, two or three numbers. So a game might go:

> Sam: 'One, two.'
>
> Kim: 'Three, four, five.'
>
> Sam: 'Six.'
>
> Kim: 'Seven, eight, nine.'
>
> Sam: 'Ten, eleven, twelve.'
>
> Kim: 'Thirteen, fourteen.'
>
> Sam: 'Fifteen, sixteen.'
>
> Kim: 'Seventeen, eighteen, nineteen.'
>
> Sam: 'Drat! Twenty.'

There is a strategy to win, but it's far from obvious and children like trying to discover it. The aim of course is to get to nineteen, because then your opponent has to say twenty.

But how can you be sure to get to nineteen? By getting to fifteen, because whatever your opponent says, 'Sixteen' or 'Sixteen, seventeen' or 'Sixteen, seventeen, eighteen', you can always get from there to nineteen.

The game is easily adapted – you can change the target from twenty to thirty, you can count up in twos instead of ones, and you can even add a third player if you want to make the game particularly vicious.

You can play this anywhere, including the car (though it does need a bit of concentration).

32

Times-Table Donk

Will your child be able to answer the question before their head donks?

Helps with: Times tables and other mental arithmetic.

Strange as it may seem, some children find it much easier to focus on mental maths tasks when they are doing something physical. This game is a great example – though you need to be strong enough (or your child small enough) to lift them up on your shoulders. As you plod around your home, or down the street, child aloft, you pose questions. 'What is three plus five?' or 'What is ten divided by two?' They have to answer correctly before you get to the next door frame or lamp-post, otherwise they risk a gentle donk on the head. Of course you and they know that you aren't actually going to allow this to happen, but the pretended terror of working out the answer as that door frame or lamp-post approaches will thrill them. You may well find your child saying, 'Wait, wait, just let me work it out,' which is of course fine.

If they are too heavy to lift, or they don't like heights, there are other ways to make times tables dynamic. One is to play catch. Toss a ball and call out a calculation at the same time: 'What's four times nine?' Surprisingly, by getting your child to focus on this physical activity you might well find they are also more focused on the mental activity of calculating.

33

Lip-Sync

Can you and your child chant a table in unison?

Helps with: Times tables.

This is another fun way to practise times tables. Choose a times table that you are going to recite together. Rehearse saying the table as 'one voice', that is, in perfect time with each other: it helps to sit facing each other.

'One seven is seven.

Two sevens are fourteen.

Three sevens are twenty one . . .'

and so on.

Seven eights are fifty-six!

Once you are both confident chanting the table in unison, one of you starts to recite the table, solo. Suppose you start. At any stage you can point at your child, stop chanting and they have to pick up reciting the table from there. They can then point and 'hand' the chant back at any other stage. How seamlessly can you both do this?

Another challenge is for one of you to be the leader of the chant — determining the speed and/or volume. Can you keep in time with each other ?

Pat-a-Cake

Put some rhythm into number patterns

Helps with: Counting in twos, fives, tens, etc.

'Pat-a-cake' counting with your child is an easy and amusing way to pass some time while you are waiting for the bath to run, or the dinner is in the oven. Facing each other you individually clap your hands together and then slap both of each other's hands. When you can do this smoothly, add in a counting pattern that you both say (in unison) when you are slapping each other's hands. For example, clap, five, clap, ten, clap, fifteen . . .

Take it in turns to be leader – that person controls the speed of the clapping. Can you keep up with each other?

Fizz Buzz

A counting game in which you have to keep your wits about you

Helps with: Learning three- and five-times tables (or any other tables come to that), and dividing.

Take it in turns to count, starting at one. Whenever you come to a number that is in the three-times table, you have to say the word 'fizz' instead of the number. And whenever you come to a number that's in the five-times table, you have to say 'buzz' instead. So a game will start: 'One . . . two . . . fizz . . . four . . . buzz . . . fizz . . . Seven . . .'

If a number is divisible by three and five, then you have to say 'fizzbuzz'. So fifteen becomes 'fizzbuzz'.

It's easy to play different versions of this game. For example, you can make it more challenging by adding the rule that you have to say 'fizz' if the number is in the three-times table OR if the number features a three. So thirteen becomes 'fizz' as well. And of course you can change which times tables you use, or even add in an extra one: for example you could have a third word – 'boloney' – for numbers in the seven-times table.

Instead of always starting from one, you can add to the challenge by starting at a larger number, such as twenty or even one hundred.

I Have a Secret Rule

What is the rule that turns their input into your output?

Helps with: Spotting patterns, confidence with arithmetic.

Choose a simple rule that you are going to apply to any number that is given to you, and keep it to yourself. For example, your secret rule might be 'I double and add one', so if you are given the number ten then your response is twenty-one, and if you are given one half then your response is two. The game is to work out what each other's rules are.

This is easily adapted to suit your child's maths strength. The rule can be as simple as 'I add two every time' or much more sophisticated, for example, 'I always round to the nearest multiple of six,' or 'I always square your number and take away five.' Or you can even have sneaky rules like 'If you give me an odd number I add ten, but if you give me an even number I take away one.'

To add a bit of fun, you can put on a synthesised computer voice. So if you're given the number five and the rule is to double and add one, you say, 'Com-pu-ter out-put...e-le-ven.'

This game works both ways round — you can invent a rule that your child has to work out, and they can do the same to you. Either way, it's great for strengthening arithmetic.

37

Guess My Shape

A mathematical mash-up of Twenty Questions and I-spy

Helps with: Developing mathematical language, geometry.

You can play this anywhere – but the car is the traditional place for I-spy.

As in the normal I-spy game, look around to choose an object, but try to pick one with obvious geometrical shapes in it, for example a pylon or a bottle.

Your child has twenty questions to find out what object you are thinking of. Each question must be about its shape and can only be answered 'Yes' or 'No', so 'Does it have a curve in it?' is fine, but 'How many sides does it have?' is not. If they correctly guess before they've used twenty questions (and each guess counts as a question) they win.

Can You Find My Number?

Guess the number by using a clever strategy

Helps with: Logic and understanding different types of number.

Choose a number within a certain range, for example, between 1 and 100. Your child has to guess the number in (say) ten goes, with yes/no answers.

You can help them to come up with questions that are good eliminators. For example, 'Is your number even?' removes half of all possibilities. Young players will need help appreciating that a no answer can be just as helpful as a yes one: 'Is your number even?' 'No' does not need to be followed up with 'Is your number odd?' (As long as you are sticking to whole numbers, of course!)

39

Pointless Maths

Find answers that others wouldn't think of

Helps with: Any maths ideas you want your child to strengthen, from arithmetic to factors.

You can play this game anywhere – at home, standing in a queue, in the car – though it's better when you have eye contact and free use of your hands.

As in the popular BBC TV show, the aim of the game is to end up with as few points as possible.

Ask a maths question that could have several answers. For example, 'Give me a number in the seven-times table.' Their answer has to be correct, but the number of points they get depends on how unusual their answer is. (You have to decide this yourself, so you need to think on your feet.) So if they say 'fourteen,' then it's a correct answer, but lots of people would think of that, so they score, maybe, 95 points out of 100. If they say 'fifty-six,' that's a much rarer answer, so maybe 25 points. And if they say, 'seven thousand, one hundred and forty-seven' – after all, the times tables don't end at twelve – then that definitely deserves to be pointless.

Other good pointless maths challenges would be:

- 'Factors of the number sixty' (i.e. whole numbers that divide exactly into sixty – common answers would be ten or six, rarer answers are twelve and fifteen).

- 'Different ways of saying one half' (e.g. fifty per cent, 0.5, two quarters, or 100 divided by 200.)

- Prime numbers.

And so on. Pointless maths can be great fun, but don't overdo it. It can be better to pose general knowledge questions and just throw in the occasional maths question.

Who Wants to be a Mathionaire

As the questions get harder, the prize money goes up . . .

Helps with: Any maths you want your child to practise, from times tables to geometry.

Like the TV game show with a very similar name, this is a game which starts with small prizes but ends on a jackpot. The jackpot need not be huge — in fact we'd advise it should be no more than 20p. It's the excitement of getting there that matters. Decide what you want the game to focus on — the times tables, for example — start on a very small prize like a fraction of a penny, and make the first question really easy. 'For one tenth of a penny — what is two times four?' When they get it right, say, 'OK, the prize has gone up to half a penny — what is five times four?' To add to the drama, when they come up with an answer say, 'Is that your final answer?' and only confirm they are right when they have done the 'Yes, final answer' bit. As the prize heads up to 5p or 10p your child can of course 'take the money' but chances are they'll want to keep heading for the jackpot. The final question should be suitably challenging: 7×8 or 12×9 (depending on where they are with their tables). As a final twist, before revealing the answer, you should of course do the trusted old: 'And the answer is . . . *coming up after the break.*'

Multiplying by Eleven

A neat way to do lightning arithmetic in your head

Helps with: Mental arithmetic.

Everyone knows the eleven-times table: it's easy. Five elevens are fifty-five, eight elevens are eighty-eight. But what about multiplying eleven by the numbers higher than ten?

What's twenty-six times eleven? Here's the secret: add together the two digits of the number (2 + 6 = 8 in this case) and put the total in the middle: 2 8 6. And that's the answer, 286!

Try another. What's sixty-one times eleven? 6 + 1 = 7, so the answer is 671.

Contain your excitement.

What is forty-eight times eleven? 4 + 8 = 12, so that makes . . . 4 12 8. That can't be right. Yes, there's a bit of a catch to this little trick. If the two digits add to ten or more, you have to be careful – the '1' needs to be added to the first digit, so the correct answer is 528.

Children do enjoy this trick; it gives them an instant thrill to have the power to do big calculations. However, as is often the case with these 'shortcut' calculation tricks, most of their value is in getting your child thinking about *why* the trick works.

(On the subject of eleven, you can demonstrate how you have eleven fingers by counting them, starting on one hand: 'Ten, nine, eight, seven, six.' Then raise the other hand: 'And five here. Six plus five is eleven.')

42

Finger Multiplication

An ancient method for doing times tables

Helps with: Number confidence.

Hold your hands in front of you, with thumbs at the top, little fingers at the bottom. Number the fingers on each hand from six to ten (thumbs are six, little fingers ten).

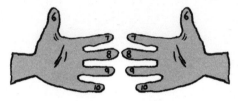

Here's how to do your times tables. Want to work out 7 × 8? Join finger seven on your left hand to finger eight on your right hand (as in the diagram below). You now have the top fingers (the ones that are touching plus those that are above them), and the bottom fingers that are dangling down (we'll call these the danglies).

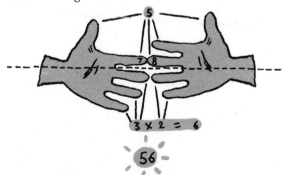

To get the answer to 7 × 8, add up the top fingers (**five**) and multiply together the danglies (three on the left times two on the right = **six**). Five six... fifty-six.

Now try 6 × 9. Join finger six on the left hand to finger nine on the right. There are now **five** top fingers and one times four = **four** danglies, answer five four... fifty-four.

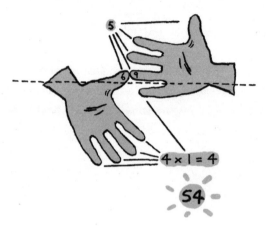

This finger shortcut was commonly used by tradesmen across Europe from the 1500s. These days, sensibly, we tend to just memorise our times tables – but it's still fun to discover other ways of doing it.

Maths at Home

There are some maths games and activities that
work best at home. Some of the ideas in this section
might require some small purchases (the Graffiti
Wall, tape measure, dartboard and clock) but these
will create opportunities for spontaneous maths that
will pay back the investment many times over.

43

Graffiti Wall

Have somewhere you can write and draw together

Helps with: Sharing maths thoughts when you are working things out or explaining.

It would be great if all maths could be done mentally, so that you could casually do it as a part of everyday conversation. But that's not the way maths is – much of it requires you to write things down. The trouble is, as soon as writing is involved, children begin to feel this is like the classroom, or doing homework, and they clam up. But there is a way to make writing maths more casual, and that is to have a space on the wall where you can scribble your ideas and workings *together*. The best place for this is probably in the kitchen, or wherever you eat meals together.

Perhaps you already have a bit of wall where you scribble ideas – a wipe-off board where you jot down shopping lists. But these tend to be a bit small. Really what you want is something that's at least a metre square, so there's space for pictures, numbers and words that can be seen at a distance. If you don't already have a space like this (and to be fair, hardly any homes do!), then you should think about creating one.

One easy way to do this is to buy a roll of lining paper. Tape a strip of the paper to the back of the kitchen door, and stick on a black felt tip using a blob of Blu-Tack. When the paper is filled up, replace it with a fresh piece. You can put the new sheet on top of the old one, so you can all look back at previous scribblings.

We've seen several homes where a solid door, or a rectangle of wall, is painted black to become a blackboard. It's often used for reminders and it's a great place for children to draw pictures, but in addition it can also be a place where all of you can jot down mathematical workings and diagrams.

If chalk is too messy, there are whiteboards with coloured pens designed to be stuck on kitchen walls. Or pens that write on glass.

Of course setting this up isn't a five-minute job. There's a trip to IKEA and some DIY involved. But when you have done it, you open up the chance for unlimited casual and spontaneous maths jottings thereafter.

And if that still feels like too much effort, we've met one family who use the side of their fridge as a write-on/wipe-off board (with the pens and a wiper stuck on the fridge with magnets).

44

Kitchen Clock

Make telling the time a routine joint activity

♟♟♟♟♟

Helps with: Learning to tell the time. Analogue clocks also help with the five-times table.

There was a time back in the 1960s when almost every home had an analogue clock (i.e. the big hand/little hand variety) in the kitchen or other main dining room. But when we made an informal survey of modern parents only about one third said they had such a clock at home.

Why are there so few analogue clocks these days? Because the world has moved on: there's a digital clock on the oven, and we've all got watches or a smartphone to tell the time, and there's a clock on the radio, so hey, who needs a kitchen clock?

Well, actually, maybe every family does. We don't think it's a coincidence that teachers tell us many of the children who enter secondary school struggle to tell the time, and particularly to work out times by adding or subtracting. ('What will the time be forty minutes from now?') Many of those children are weak at telling the time because they are so inexperienced at doing it. (Most adults are OK at telling the time. Is this because they are better at maths than their children? No, it's simply that they have done it so many times.)

If you have an analogue clock on the wall at home, telling the time becomes a shared experience. In the morning you can look up at the clock and say to your child: 'Look, we have to be out of the house by half past eight – you've got six minutes to get your coat and shoes on.' Or instead of telling them, find ways of getting them to work it out for themselves.

If your child is just beginning to tell the time, you can stick Post-its around the outside of the clock with the minutes past the hour on 5, 10, 15 . . . 45, 50, 55. Labelling the minutes helps them to see that there are two scales on a clock face – hours and minutes.

45

How Tall Are You Now?

Children love to watch themselves grow

Helps with: Measurement, the conversion from metric to imperial.

Choose a vertical strip on the inside of a door frame or a cupboard door as the place where you are going to measure your child's height. Every four or five months, measure their height, mark it with a horizontal line and put the date against it. Then get your child to use a tape measure to find out how tall they are. Even better, if you have an old tape measure – one that has both centimetres and feet/inches is ideal – attach it to your designated door frame so it is permanently there. This makes it easy to read off height quickly, without the hassle of looking for the measure.

The reason why having imperial measures is useful is that most people – adults and children – still talk about height in feet. 'He was six feet tall, dark and handsome.' Rarely do you hear it being reported that 'He was around 180 centimetres, dark and handsome.' So even though at school your child will be dealing almost exclusively in metric measures, familiarity with both types is really handy. And what better way than through measuring their height, something that most children find endlessly fascinating as they grow up.

If you've got another tape measure around, young children are intrigued to find that measuring how long they are when lying down turns out to be the same as their height when standing up.

If you think you'll be moving home, you can make the strip where you record heights out of something that's easily transplanted – a flexible measuring tape, for example. At the very least, before you move make a note of what the last height was, so you're ready to mark it on a doorway at the new home.

46

How Many Feet?

Use feet to measure lengths

Helps with: Understanding measurement.

Whenever you have an excuse to do some measuring, get your child involved. For example, when you're getting a new carpet you need to measure how big the room is. And while using a tape measure is great, why not resort to a more ancient measurement – your feet.

'Did you know that the Romans used to measure distances in feet? And feet meant the length of their feet. So let's do the same thing.'

Walk across your room, one foot in front of the other, counting how many feet that is. 'Well, it seems that this room is about twelve feet across. Can you just check that for me?' Your child will now discover that using their feet, it's more like eighteen feet across. Hmm, when people measure in feet, which feet do they mean?

How long is a 'real' foot? If you have a ruler to hand, check. How does yours compare?

And here's a thing: most people are between six and seven feet tall. Six of their own feet, that is.

(If you want to continue on this theme, there's a lovely children's story called *How Big Is a Foot* by Rolf Myller. It makes a good bedtime story.)

47

Kids' Darts

A game that makes mental arithmetic routine

Helps with: Mental arithmetic, doubling, trebling, meeting a target.

Although you can put up a dartboard in your child's bedroom, or in the garage if you have one, it's best to have a board in a family space like the lounge or the inside of the front door (so you need one that easily hangs on a hook or door handle, for example).

We are not endorsing a normal adult dartboard here. For one thing, hitting those segments is hard enough for adults, let alone children. (And there are issues over those sharp pointy things, too.)

So instead, invest in a magnetic or Velcro board, preferably one in which the number segments at which you aim are bigger than on a standard board. If it doesn't have 'double' and 'treble' features, invent them. Announce that 'Odd numbers count double,' for example. Set a target of, say, one hundred and have in mind a nice reward for the winner: 'First one to get to one hundred gets first choice when we open that new box of chocolates.' Your child has to keep their own score while you keep yours.

The target can be either to get over 100 points or – more like real darts – you can make the rule that the winner is the one who ends on *exactly* 100. Of course in normal darts you start at a high number (such as 301 or 501) and the aim is to reduce your total to 0 by subtracting your score. Tougher again, you have to finish on a double. That's even better practice of mental arithmetic, if your child is ready for it.

48

Upstairs Downstairs

Going up and down steps can be more than just one, two, three

Helps with: Confidence in counting (and more advanced, it helps with multiples, division and factors – even prime numbers).

When your child is going upstairs with you, make it a habit to count out loud the number of stairs you climb. Going up, count from one up to the top stair, which might be thirteen, for example. Going down, remember what the top number is, and count down from that. The stairs become your very own household number line.

When the stair numbers are familiar, you can start playing games like 'Halfway up' (remember Kermit's nephew Robin who sang A. A. Milne's poem 'Halfway down the stairs is a stair where I sit'.) With your child, discover which of your stairs is the halfway one. You can discover together that if you have an even number of stairs (such as twelve) then there is an exact halfway stair (in this case, number six – you can go up six stairs or down six stairs from there). If you have an odd number of stairs, like thirteen, the halfway stair is between numbers six and seven.

Another staircase game you can play is 'Giant steps'. What happens if you go up two stairs at a time? Now you count

two, four, six, eight ... if you have a total of twelve stairs, then giant steps of two at a time, or three, or four, will all get you exactly to the top stair. But giant steps of five (if you could do them) would get you to stair ten, with two left over.

If you have thirteen stairs, on the other hand, there don't seem to be any giant steps you can do to land exactly on the top stair. Two doesn't work (one left over), nor does three (ditto) or four (ditto); for five steps there are three left over, and so on. Hmm, there's something special about thirteen. What is it? Answer – it is a prime number. It doesn't divide by anything other than one or itself. So there's only one giant step that will work on a thirteen staircase: to climb up thirteen steps in one go.

Once you and your child have got the hang of this, you can use it wherever you encounter stairs together: when you are out and about, on the Tube or at train stations, etc.

49

Screen Time

Children value things more when there's a limit

Helps with: Working out time, mental calculation – and managing TV addiction!

If you're tired of your child watching too much TV, then announce that as an experiment you are going to ration it. They will be allowed to watch no more than, say, one hour. So it's up to them to look at the TV schedules for the day, and work out which programmes they want to watch. For each programme they are interested in, they need to know how long the episode is, and add up the times. Set up a timer (on your phone?) that you switch on whenever they are watching, and switch off when they stop. When it occurs to you, you can show them the timer, and leave them to work out how much time they have left.

It's a great way of getting them to work with times and schedules, and who knows, it might even have a long-term impact on their TV-viewing habits.

You can do something similar with playing computer games, though in this case, the duration of most games is unlimited, so the only mathematical skill you'll be asking of them is how long they have left. For example, if you've allocated two hours and your timer says thirty-two minutes, they have one hour twenty-eight minutes' playtime left today.

And of course you can combine all the above and just have a limit on total screen time, whether that's TV, computer or phone.

If your phone doesn't have a timer, use the one on the oven or microwave.

50

What's the Score?

Work out the score before the TV tells you

Helps with: Quick addition.

There are lots of occasions when scores pop up on television. In sport, there are scores for football, tennis, gymnastics, cricket and rugby (to name but a few), and in many talent shows such as *Strictly Come Dancing* and *Dancing on Ice* the judges' marks are totted up to give an overall score.

A simple challenge when watching with your child is to work out the score before it flashes on the screen. The four judges hold up their marks: Six! Six! Seven! Seven! Quick, what's the total?

In football keeping up the score is pretty trivial – only one goal is scored at a time, so the score 1-1 will change to 2-1. But in rugby where more points are on offer, the challenge is more interesting. Wales leads France by 14 points to 10 and they then score a try. What's the score now? You get 5 points for a try, $14 + 5 = 19$, so the score is now 19-10. What would France need to get back level? They need 9 points. It's 3 points for a penalty, so three penalties would do it. And a converted try (7 points) plus a penalty (3 points) would be enough to put them ahead.

You can do some intelligent guessing, too, and see who gets closest. 'I think Celebrity X is going to get 31 points in

Strictly, what do you think?' 'What do you reckon the full-time score in this match is going to be?'

Another routine calculation in football matches is to work out how many minutes are left in the game. With 73 minutes gone, you can casually ask, 'We need an equaliser, how long is there still to play?' Subtracting 73 from 90 is good mental arithmetic. And there's always injury time to calculate as well.

Mealtimes

While lots of the ideas elsewhere in the book are great to do when sitting around for a meal, the ideas in this section are all directly linked to preparing for or sitting at a meal.

Cereal Count

Estimation at breakfast

Helps with: Counting, estimation.

At breakfast, get your child to pour their dried cereal into their bowl and then guess how many Shreddies, Cheerios or other cereal of your choice there are in the bowl. You and anyone else at the breakfast table can join in too. If you have time, you can count the pieces before you eat them. If not, keep a tally as you eat (this probably means adding clumps of five or six to the total at a time). Whoever is closest wins. If there are two or more of you at the table, before you start you can try to guess which of you has the most in your bowl, and then check.

On a busy day, this is probably only going to work if it's a cereal with big pieces when you might typically have fewer than twenty in your bowl. Rice Krispies are for lazy Sunday mornings (or those occasions when you want to keep your child occupied for a while).

Meeting the Deadline

If your child wants to be the next Gordon Ramsay . . .

Helps with: Timekeeping, counting forward and back on clocks. Timetables.

This is good to try at the weekend, when you're preparing a roast or baking. Ask your child to help you with your timings – for example, how long it will take to roast a chicken. Read the cooking instructions, which will tell you how long the meal needs to cook for. Let's suppose the instructions say, 'Roast the chicken for 1 hour 45 minutes at Gas Mark 5.'

Tell your cooking assistant that you want to eat at 6 p.m., and ask them what time the chicken needs to go into the oven.

You can practise calculating back from a deadline away from the kitchen too. Journeys are great for this, especially if it's a journey to somewhere your child is keen to go. For example, suppose you are off to see their favourite cousin Chloe. You need to get the train. The plan is that Aunt Maggie will meet you at the station sometime around 7 p.m.

Sit with your child as you look up train times, ask them to help you find the time of the train that arrives at Aunt Maggie's station around 7 p.m. When you know what time you have to get to your station, work back from that to see when you need to leave home. For example, maybe you need to catch the bus, and allow thirty minutes to get to the station. And maybe it takes about five minutes to get from home to the bus stop.

Try not to set this as a 'test' for your child. (They may resent this, and ask, 'Why can't you work it out yourself?') Instead, ensure that you involve them in the planning, ask them to help you look up the cooking or train times, play a little dumb and be slow to work things out to give them a chance to help you.

Pizza Fractions

Show why two sixths equal one third

Helps with: Understanding fractions, including adding fractions and equivalent fractions.

This works best with whole pizzas, for example the ones that you cook from frozen, because the idea is that you will get your child to do the slicing, or at least show you where to slice.

Start with questions like 'How many of us will be eating?' and 'How big should the slices be?'

Even if the pizza is only being shared by two people, it's normal to divide it into several slices. So a pizza for two can be divided into sixths (three pieces each) or eighths (four each). This is a natural way of showing that a half is the same as two quarters, three sixths and four eighths.

Sharing between three people you get two sixths (one third) each.

Dividing up isn't restricted to pizzas, of course, though they do have the nice feature of (a) being round, and (b) usually being completely eaten in one meal. Cakes can be cut up into fractions too (if you want to make eight slices, cut into quarters, then halve all the quarters).

Wacky Quarters

Be creative when cutting up toast and sandwiches

Helps with: Understanding that fractions don't always have to look the same.

The nice thing about toast — square toast at least — is that there are three natural ways to divide it into four quarters: down and across, diagonally, and four strips:

And if you want to go wild, any pair of lines at right angles that go through the centre of a slice of toast will make four wacky but identical quarters. For example this:

Cutlery Challenge

Make triangles with knives, forks and spoons

Helps with: Geometry and thinking about properties of triangles.

Set the challenge of creating a triangle using items of cutlery and anything else with a fairly straight edge around the table – knives, forks, a placemat.

Now for the points. Award one point for a triangle in which all three angles are smaller than right angles. Three points for a triangle with one angle that is bigger than a right angle. And five points for a triangle which has a right angle. The right angle doesn't have to be precisely 90 degrees, it just has to be close enough. You can use a credit card or the corner of a napkin to check the angle.

What happens if the three objects won't form a triangle? No points for that – but when might this happen? You can't make a triangle if the longest side is bigger than the two other sides added together. Two teaspoons usually add to less than the side of a menu, for example.

Chatty Jar

Random prompts for a quick conversation about maths

Helps with: Language, mathematical imagination.

This does need a bit of preparation but it's something you can use again and again round the family table. Write twenty to thirty thought-provoking questions on slips of paper and pop them in a jar.

At one of those mealtimes when you have time to talk, pick a question out of the jar at random. The questions should be fun and not too high-minded, and do have a wide range of questions – not all maths-related! Here are some maths ones to get you started:

- If a square has four sides, a pentagon has five sides and so on, how many sides does a circle have?

- What's the biggest number ever?

- What's the longest pole you could fit in this room and where would it fit?

- If a spider wanted to walk from this window to that wall, what would be its shortest route?

- Which fits better, a square peg in a round hole, or a round peg in a square hole?

- If you had £5 and needed to have a meal, what would you buy to last the longest?

- How long would it take to count to a million?

- Would we count differently if we had four fingers on each hand instead of five?

- If we all wanted to shake hands with each other how many handshakes is that?

- When you are Mum's age, how old will Mum be?

- When will you be half Daddy's age?

Doing the Shopping

Shopping trips provide plenty of opportunities to play
with money and also to spot mathematical patterns.

Supermarket Challenge

It's never too early to learn about shopping bills

Helps with: Estimation, comparing numbers, making connections with school arithmetic and real-life calculation.

When you take your child to the supermarket or out shopping for food, there are lots of ways that you can work in useful maths. If you don't care about the brand, a simple instruction is, 'Can you find me the cheapest tin of beans?'

Another handy game is to keep a running total of roughly how much the shopping costs so far. To make it simple, you can suggest rounding the price of everything to the nearest £1, or 50p. When you get to the till, both of you have to guess what the final bill will be, and whoever is closest wins ... whatever prize you think is fitting for the moment.

Deal or No Deal?

Investigate supermarket prices and find the best deal

Helps with: Understanding ratios, division.

Supermarkets are sometimes accused of dodgy practices when offering 'deals' to customers. Your child can help to be a sleuth looking out for which offers really do make sense.

A 500g box of cereal might be priced at £1.80, while a 750g box is £2.50. Is that a deal? What about juice boxes priced at £2.20, or three for £5?

There's usually (but not always) help on the shelf, which might indicate what each product costs *per 100 grams*. A 750g box of cereal at £2.25 is 30p per 100g, while a 500g box at £1.80 is 36p. That makes the 750g box a better deal – as long as you plan to eat that much of the cereal, of course.

This can open up into a more interesting investigation. What is the cheapest or most expensive food in the supermarket that your child can find? To do this, foods will need to be priced on weight. What's the cheapest 100g of food they can find? And what is the most expensive? They might need to convert price per kilograms into price per 100g for some of the weightier foods like potatoes. And if the supermarket hasn't done the calculation for them, they might need to work out the answer in their heads. (Zequals can be handy for this – see page 31.)

Child in a Sweet Shop

Sweets can be one of the best motivators for handling money

Helps with: Mental arithmetic and rapid juggling of numbers to fit a target.

Try this if you have an old-fashioned sweetie shop where you live. Or a shop, such as a newsagent, where there are individual sweets that cost 10p or less, and where the prices are marked clearly – as long as the shopkeeper is happy.

Give your child a sum of money, £2 say, to buy sweets. Tell them they are allowed to spend as much as they want but if there is any change you want it back. That's a good incentive to spend as close to £2 as they can. This works even better if they go with a sibling or one or more friends with each child getting £2, because they will collaborate in their calculations. If they are younger than eight you should probably accompany them, so that you can steer them if they are completely stuck.

If it's obvious that they have overspent, let them know. When they think they've got £2 worth they should go to the till. If they've overspent then tough, they have to put something back. If a child ends up with change then they can always top up with more; underspending is a good lesson in knowing how to get the most from a budget.

Robot Dad (or Mum)

Be a robot when you return home with the shopping

Helps with: Learning to do coding, the importance of accurate instructions, angles and measurements.

This is a great game to play when you've just got home from doing the shopping, loaded with bags.

As you step in through the door with a bag of shopping, tell your child that you are now a robot, and you need instructions for taking the contents to the kitchen. Even better if there's something that has to go to a specific place: for example, the milk has to go into the fridge. The instructions the robot needs from your child are things like 'Go forward three paces,' 'Turn left,' and so on.

When your child gives you instructions, deliberately take them literally and in such a way that things 'go wrong' very quickly. So if they say, 'Go forward,' start going forward quickly at the angle you were originally pointing, so that you bump into a wall or stairs and are now helplessly stepping up and down pressed against the radiator. In a robot voice, say things like 'HELP, I NEED MORE ACCURATE INSTRUCTIONS,' 'HOW MANY STEPS SHOULD I GO?' 'WHAT SIZE OF STEP?' 'WHAT ANGLE SHOULD I TURN?' 'CLOCKWISE OR ANTICLOCKWISE?' etc.

If you have two or more children, you can get one to be the robot and another to give instructions. But it might help for you to be the robot first so they know what to expect.

61

The Big Count

Work out how many things there are in the supermarket

Helps with: Multiplication and estimation.

Supermarkets are full of things arranged in orderly patterns, but there's no time to count them all. Instead, you can encourage your child to try to work out quantities. The questions you can tackle together are limitless, for example:

- If this supermarket car park was full, how many cars would there be? (Count the number of rows and the number of cars per row.)

- How many toilet rolls have they got here?

If you want to be more adventurous, you can find ways to tie those calculations back to your everyday life.

- How long would it take us to *use* all those toilet rolls?

Unless your child is a wizard at mental arithmetic, there's only time to do estimates. This is where Zequals (page 31) can be a very handy tool. 'There are twenty-three cars per row (that zequals twenty) and eighteen rows (that zequals twenty) . . . so the total zequals twenty times twenty equals four hundred cars in the full car park.'

On a Journey

These games are particularly suited to when you are on a road or rail journey, with plenty of time spent looking out of the window as the world goes by.

62

Number Treasure Hunt

Collect numbers in order, starting at one

Helps with: Number recognition, place value, equations.

At its simplest this is a game to collect the whole numbers in order from one up to whatever target you choose. These might be numbers on buildings, on road signs or on car number plates. The basic game (for the youngest children) is just to spot all the digits from one to nine in order.

For example if you are searching for the number '3' and you see number 139 on a sign, it contains the digit '3' so that counts.

In a slightly more advanced version for older children, it's the 'place value' of the number that counts. So in the number 139, the three actually represents the number 30, not 3. If you are looking for an 8, then if you spot 831 that doesn't count (the 8 represents 800) but if you spot 48 that does count. And if you are looking for 20, then in the number 4128, the 2 represents 20, so that counts too!

The most advanced version of this game is Number Formula. In this version you take any number that you spot that has at least two digits, and use all of those digits exactly once, combining them in a way that equals the number you are hunting for. For example, if you are hunting for the number '2' and spot the number 75 then you can make $7 - 5 = 2$.

If you are hunting for '6' and you spot 472 then...hmm, tricky...but one of you might spot that $42 \div 7 = 6$.

You can make this game as complicated as you want, allowing all the functions you'd find on a calculator such as square root and brackets.

Are We There Yet?

*Make the countdown for the rest of your journey
more exciting*

🯄🯄🯄🯄🯄

Helps with: Estimation.

This is good for any long journey, but particularly one in a car. 'When will we be there?' The moans sometimes start when the long trek is barely thirty minutes old. Start a contest that everyone can enter. This can be either:

- Who can get closest to predicting the number on the milometer when we get to the destination?

Or:

- Who can be closest to the exact time when we stop the car at our destination?

If you have a satnav then it can of course give you its own opinion on both the arrival time and the mileage. But that's OK, because satnavs are never perfect, and they can't predict that wrong turning you take, or your diversion into Tesco to buy a snack. So it's fine for the satnav to play as well, but you have to remember what its guess was when you started the game – it does have a habit of changing its mind!

How Many Wheels on That Wagon?

A game of lorry spotting

Helps with: Working out an answer when you can't count.

Big trucks have lots of wheels, but normally you can't see all of them. The ones on the far side are hidden. Pick a number – twelve, for example – and say that you will award points to the first person to spot a lorry that has twelve wheels. It will quickly dawn on your child that they have to work out a way of counting the wheels they can't see. They'll probably realise that as long as they can count the wheels on one side, they simply have to double that number to get the total – but if they don't spot that, give them a hint.

What's nice about lorry wheels is that they come in different combinations. Sometimes there's one at the front and two at the back, sometimes two and two. And on bigger lorries you'll also get double wheels (that's two wheels side by side), so even counting up those on one side needs some care.

Pub Cricket

Turn a car or bus journey into a game of cricket

🎳🎳🎳🎳🎳

Helps with: Addition.

This game works better in built-up areas than in the countryside. And it doesn't work at all on the motorway.

There are lots of possible ways to play this, so we've given a few suggestions for rules – but feel free to adapt them.

Decide who is going to 'bat' first. Let's call that person 'the batsman'. Every time you go past a pub, look at the name. If it includes a person or creature that has legs, then the batsman's score goes up by the number of legs. So if you go past the Goose and Granite, the batsman gets two runs, and it's the same for the Lord Nelson (remember, he had two legs, even though he only had one arm). The Dog and Duck scores six. And if you're lucky enough to go past Ye Olde Centipede then that's a hundred runs, but we've yet to see a pub with that name. You might need to act as umpire when it comes to the Horse and Hounds – make an upper limit of ten runs per pub, perhaps? And for names like the King's Head, decide in advance if this should count as two runs because it refers to a king, even though the pub is dedicated to a different part of his body.

Some people like to have the rule that if the pub name does not involve any legs then you are out, but this tends to mean that lots of players end up making no runs. So a better rule if you want the game to last a bit longer is that pubs with no legs just count as no runs. But if the name features a plant of some sort, then the batsman is out, and the next player has a go. So you're out if the pub is the Slug and Lettuce or the Rose. The Bee and Buttercup is out, but you do score the six runs first – an example of Six and Out.

This gives a whole new meaning to the term 'getting legless at the pub', but perhaps that's not something you want to share with your child.

Green Light

Can you predict the colour of the next traffic light?

Helps with: Keeping score and understanding risk.

In this game players take it in turn to win points on passing through green traffic lights.

Choose who will take the first turn. As soon as the car passes through the next green light, the first player earns five points, and must choose to say 'Stick' or 'Twist'. If they 'Stick', they keep five points and the next player starts on the next green light. If the first player says 'Twist', you wait to see the colour of the next set of traffic lights: if it's green, the player wins another five points, and again can choose 'Stick' or 'Twist'. If however the light is red when you get to it, the player loses all the points won in that round and the next player takes a turn. And so on.

There's an interesting strategy here: should you stick on five points, or ten, or more? It depends partly on where you are: in the inner city during rush hour there are usually more red lights than out of town and outside peak hours.

(It's easy to get swept away in the excitement of this game, but remind your children that if you play it too aggressively, you might end up acquiring the wrong kind of points – from the local police.)

Stuck at the Red Light

How long will we be stuck in this queue?

Helps with: Estimation and timekeeping.

If you are a long way back in the queue, how long will it be before you get through the lights? Next time the lights turn green, count how many cars get through before they turn red. If you are twentieth in the line and it looks as though only six cars got through the lights, it's likely there will be two more red lights before you get through. (This game also works really well when you are standing in a queue; waiting to go on a theme park ride, for example. How many people are in front of you in the queue, and how many people are getting on the ride per minute?)

If physics is your thing, you can time how long it takes between the car at the front of the queue starting to move and your car starting to move. Then estimate how far it is from your car to the lights. That will tell you the speed at which the 'pulse' of moving traffic travels. Viewed from the air, this pulse of movement is a bit like a wave flowing through the traffic. (If you want to see what this wave looks like, look up videos of 'longitudinal waves' on the Web.)

68

Higher or Lower?

What will the next bus number be?

Helps with: Confidence with numbers, understanding chance.

This is a nod to Bruce Forsyth's classic show *Play Your Cards Right*. In this version, instead of turning over giant playing cards, you look out for the numbers on buses. A bus goes past and it is a 185. Will the next bus number be higher or lower? There's a bit of strategy here, but you need to know the range of bus numbers in the place where you are bus-spotting. Let's suppose the range of bus numbers is 1 to 200. A number 7 bus goes past. 'Will the next bus be higher or lower?' you ask. 'Higher,' goes the chorus on the back

seat. And the next bus is . . . a 22! Will the next be higher or lower? The aim is to make four correct predictions. (If the next bus is the same number as the previous one, ignore that bus and wait for the next one to go past.)

69

Bike Helmets

A survey to answer life's big questions

Helps with: Surveys, ratios, percentages.

This game works for any journey, though built-up areas may be better.

Do most cyclists wear helmets? Which car colour is more popular, yellow or green? These are great questions to ask, because nobody knows the answer. The way to find out is to do a survey. It can keep kids occupied for quite a while. To add a bit of spice to the survey, you can make it a contest: 'If we see a cyclist with a helmet, you get a point, but if we see one without a helmet then I get a point. Let's see who gets to twenty points first.'

By the time the game has produced a winner, you have an interesting survey result. Let's suppose cycle helmets have scored twenty and non-helmets have got to fifteen. What proportion of cyclists wear helmets? It's twenty out of thirty-five. What's that as a percentage? Twenty out of thirty-five is close to sixty out of one hundred, so this survey suggests that about sixty per cent of cyclists wear helmets – at least in the place where you do the survey.

One for a Sheep, Two for a Cow

An animal-spotting game for the car

Helps with: Mental arithmetic.

This is a really simple game and one to play when travelling through the countryside.

Decide on how many points you want to allocate to spotting different farm (and other) animals. First to spot the animals gets the points for them, and first to, say, thirty points wins.

These points seem to work:

- Sheep – one point

- Cows – two points

- Horses – five points

- Pigs – ten points

- Donkeys – twenty points

- Elephants – one thousand points (well, you don't see many of them out and about)

Only two animals in any field count, so if you see a herd of cows, that would be four points (for two cows).

If animals are in short supply, do it with car colours or types of building instead (newsagent one point, church two points, school three points, castle one hundred points).

How Fast Are We Going?

Work out your speed when you can't see a speedometer

Helps with: Understanding speeds, scaling up numbers.

It's not always possible to see a speedometer when you are travelling, but it's still possible to estimate how fast you are going. When walking, work out how far you walk for a period of, say, one minute. You'll need to know roughly how big your normal pace is (see How Many Feet? on page 81). Typically an adult's pace is just under a metre (or three feet) and a child's is perhaps half a metre (one and a half feet) but of course it depends a lot on how tall you are.

Suppose your child does one hundred paces in a minute. That's about fifty metres. And fifty metres in a minute is the same as $50 \times 60 = 3,000$ metres in an hour. Or 3 kilometres per hour.

On the road, there are other ways to check distance. Motorways have a little post every hundred metres. Count how many of those you go past in, say, one minute. Another possibility is to look at the distance signs. If you pass a sign saying 'Leicester 25 miles', start the timer, and wait a few minutes until you see the next sign to Leicester. If, six minutes later, there is a sign saying 'Leicester 18 miles' then you've covered seven miles in six minutes. How many miles is that in one hour? There are ten lots of six minutes in an hour, so you would cover ten lots of seven miles. In other words, you're travelling at 70 miles per hour.

If you are on the train, look out for mile or (increasingly) kilometre markers that are to be found on the embankment (they are often yellow or white). Count how many markers you pass in five minutes and multiply by twelve to get an estimate of your speed in miles (or kilometres) per hour.

End of the Day

These ideas all link in to the end-of-day routine: reflection on the day, bath time, stories. Late in the day is also often a good time for one-to-one chatting, and if you are low-key about it you can play some maths games too.

72

Water Play

The bath has lots of maths opportunities to tap into

Helps with: Understanding volume of different shapes.

Most children love playing with water. Bath time is the obvious opportunity to do this in a way that isn't going to get their clothes or (with any luck) the floor soaked. Make sure that among their usual bath toys you have different receptacles – a plastic saucepan and a tall thin cylinder, say. Fill up one of the objects with water to the brim, then wonder out loud if, when poured into the other one, the water is going to fill it or not. Children will often be surprised that different shapes can contain the same amount of water, or that a tall object might actually contain less water than a short fat one.

If you have an old measuring jug, add that to the bath toys. Your child can find out how many scoops of water it takes to fill up the measuring jug to the 100ml line.

If this isn't fun enough (and for many children it really is more than enough fun!) then turn it into something like those old challenges from *It's a Knockout*. Tell them they have one minute to fill up their squeezy whale with water, squirt the water out of the whale's mouth into the jug, and get the water level up to 250ml. 'Starting . . . NOW!' (You can add to the excitement by providing the musical sound effects.)

Squeezy toys can be used to see how tall a fountain you can make. Can you squirt the water higher than the taps? To the top of the shower? To the ceiling?

73

Plot of the Day

Plot a graph of how your day went, with highs and lows

Helps with: Graphs.

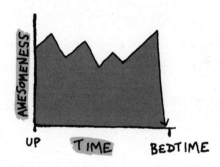

'So, what happened at school today?'

'Nothing much.'

Sounds familiar? Extracting information from your child can be extremely difficult. One way to do it is to get them to draw a graph of their day. The first time you try this, you should be in charge. Start by drawing the axes, with time of day along the bottom of the graph and 'Happiness' or 'Excitement' – whatever you want to measure – up the side.

'The day started with breakfast...how was that...a bit boring?...Then I dropped you at school and you saw your friends...a bit better...Then what was the first lesson? History – are you doing the Romans at the moment? How was that today?' Work through the day, plotting the points as you go, to end up with a chart that gives some impression of what the highlights and lowlights have been. And while it's great if this exercise does reveal some insights into your child's day, from a maths point of view it doesn't matter if they reveal much or not. If they say 'Boring' to everything that has happened in the day, then the graph will be bumping along the bottom. If everything has been fabulously exciting, the graph will be high up. Whatever the graph, it's still getting them used to the idea of presenting information in this form.

74

Personal Pie Chart

Draw a pie chart of your favourite/least favourite things

Helps with: Pie charts, proportions and percentages.

'I hate French...I love Science.' Children do have a habit of describing things in extremes. Getting them to represent all their feelings in a pie chart is a great way to get them to be more realistic about how good or bad things are – and they can learn a lot about fractions and percentages at the same time.

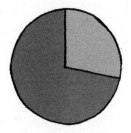

■ Time my brother spends being annoying.
□ Time my brother spends asleep.

Start by drawing a circle to represent the pie (or if you prefer, the cake). Now ask them to think of all the things they do at school and to divide the pie up into slices according to how much they like them. It might help if you give an example first by doing a diagram of how much you liked different subjects. (For example, you might make a quarter of the pie history, one eighth maths, a tiny slice for French...whatever.) Once they've divided up their cake you can comment on the different fractions. 'So I reckon about one quarter of your pie is music, that's twenty-five per cent. Interesting...'

They can do a pie chart of anything. For example, how they spent the day (what proportion was spent writing, listening, talking, playing), how they felt (happy, sad, excited), how much they liked lunch (custard ninety per cent, cabbage ten per cent) – the possibilities are endless, and the silliest ones are often the best.

Fred

A wacky introduction to algebra

Helps with: Working out unknowns.

If $3 + x = 7$, what is x? That sort of question can send shivers through many parents' spines and leave children cold. Yet the same question can become fun just by making 'x' into something silly – one of your child's teddy bears or soft toys, for example. Let's say it's a bear called Fred.

'Let's play a game of Fred,' you announce. 'Four plus two equals Fred's number – do you know what Fred's number is?'

'Six!'

'That's right. OK, let's try another. Oh dear, Fred is trying to be cunning this time. Three plus Fred equals seven. Which number is Fred this time?'

If your child is stuck, use your fingers. 'Here are three fingers . . . what do we need to add to make seven?' You can discover together that Fred's number must be four.

Pyjama Countdown

Use creative counting to get your child to beat the deadline

Helps with: Fractions and other numbers.

This is a good trick to get your child to stop dawdling and get a move on.

'It's time for bed. If you aren't upstairs by the time I've counted to ten then you're going to lose one story.' Sound familiar? Deadlines like this can be effective, but most effective if the child actually does what they have been asked to do before the deadline arrives.

Invariably, though, they will struggle to meet the strict countdown that you announce. What should you do if you've set the challenge of getting pyjamas on by the count of ten, but they've only just removed their trousers and you're already up to five? You can slow down, but why not make the counting interesting instead. 'Six . . . six and a half . . . six and three quarters . . . seven . . . seven point two . . . seven point five.' It's fun to change the counting target from time to time. Instead of counting to ten, why not count to, say, thirteen, or instead of counting up you can count down. Or count in twos or fives or even thousands.

Captain Correct

Add maths into story time

Helps with: Number sense and thinking about when maths is used.

In this game you and your child take turns to be Captain Correct – a fastidious mathematician.

The person who is not Captain Correct starts to tell a story – perhaps a classic fairy tale, or the plot of a book that you are reading together, or just what happened at school today.

As the story unfolds, Captain Correct interjects, asking for more precise mathematical details. For example:

'Once upon a time...'

CC: *'Exactly how long ago was this?'*

'One hundred and thirty years ago. A girl called Heidi...'

CC: *'How old was Heidi?'*

'Five.'

CC: *'Exactly five years old?'*

'Five and a half. She set off to visit Peter.'

CC: *'What time did she leave home?'*

And so on...

Games with Simple Props

So far we've kept the games and activities as simple as possible. Some of the games in this section will need just a bit of preparation such as digging out a pack of cards or the Snakes and Ladders board.

Triple Snakes and Ladders

The traditional game — but three times faster

You will need: Ordinary board games, with dice.

Helps with: Early adding and multiplication skills.

Triple Snakes and Ladders is just like the traditional game, but after rolling the die, instead of moving on that number of spaces, you go *three times* as many. Roll a one and you go forward three, roll a six and you go forward a whopping eighteen. This is a great way of developing your child's three-times table — and, sneakily, the game is finished three times as quickly. Win-win.

Other games that are ripe for speeding up are:

- Monopoly — deal out all the property cards at the start, so your only concern will be buying houses and hotels and extracting or paying rent.

- Snap — If you get to the end of the pile and there's not been a snap then tough, end of game.

- Bingo — You can cross off the number called out or a number that's ten bigger or smaller, so if number 23 is called, you can also remove 13 and 33.

Attention!

A card game that makes subtraction fun

You will need: A pack of playing cards and three players.

Helps with: Arithmetical skills.

This is a game for three players. You can play it anywhere, but you need to be seated so you can see each other.

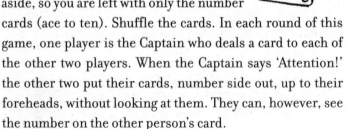

Remove all the picture cards and set them aside, so you are left with only the number cards (ace to ten). Shuffle the cards. In each round of this game, one player is the Captain who deals a card to each of the other two players. When the Captain says 'Attention!' the other two put their cards, number side out, up to their foreheads, without looking at them. They can, however, see the number on the other person's card.

The Captain adds the two numbers on the cards and says the total – for example, if the Captain can see five and seven she says, 'Twelve.' The other players each have to work out what number is on their own card. A point is awarded to the person who gets the correct answer first. And if that becomes too easy, then the Captain can multiply the two numbers on the cards together.

80

Hit the Target

A running-total game to practise adding and taking away

You will need: A pack of playing cards.

Helps with: Arithmetical skills.

Take the picture cards out of the pack and set them to one side. Shuffle the remaining cards and place them face down between you and your child.

Decide on a target number, for example twenty-five.

Take it in turns to flip over the top card and place it in a face-up pile. Let's suppose you go first and turn over an eight. Now your child turns over a six, so they call the total, fourteen. You next turn over three, and say, 'Seventeen.'

If a card turned over takes the running total over twenty-five, then that player must subtract its value. So, if the running total is twenty-three and you turn over four you say, 'Nineteen.' If the next card is, say, a two, the play reverts to adding, but if it was, say, a nine, you must again subtract. The winner is the player to correctly say, 'Twenty-five.' (Shuffle the face-up cards and turn them face down if they run out before anyone gets there.)

Of course, there is nothing particularly special about twenty-five as the winning total, so choose any target number you like – though it's probably best if the number is no higher than fifty.

81

Three in a Row

A simple game with intriguing tactics

You will need: Paper and a pencil.

Helps with: Thinking strategically.

Mark fifteen dots in a row on the piece of paper.

Take it in turns to cross out one of the dots.

The winner is the first person to create three crossed-out dots in a row. It doesn't matter which player has crossed out the other two; they just have to be adjacent crosses, that is, no unwanted dots between any of them, as below:

This is a really quick game, but the tactics are interesting, as you'll discover if you play it a couple of times. If you cross out a dot next to another that's crossed out, you've lost: the other player can make a row of three. But you also lose if you cross out a dot that is two away from another, because your opponent will cross out the one in the middle.

If it's your turn in the game shown overleaf, what should you do? (Clue: you've lost!)

'Hmm, which dot should I cross out next?'

Is it better to go first or second? Where's the best first move? It isn't obvious.

Like the game of Twenty (see page 56) this game is easily varied. Instead of fifteen dots you can choose any number from five dots upwards. And instead of the aim being to get three in a row, you can make it four or more.

82

Bean Grab

Multiplication and division is more than a hill of beans

You will need: Some dried beans, small dried pasta or counters.

Helps with: Factors and multiples.

Players take it in turns to grab a handful of beans (or whatever counting materials you have to hand).

The challenge is to arrange the beans into piles of the same number with none left over. There must be at least two beans in a pile. Let's suppose the first player grabbed twenty beans. They can make five piles of four beans.

The next player then sees if they can arrange the same number of beans into new piles that don't have four in each. Four piles of five, for example. That scores two points.

Play keeps passing between the players for as long as different arrangements can be found. The score doubles for each new arrangement: two piles of ten, that's four points. Ten piles of two, that's eight points. When players agree that they have run out of possibilities it is the next person's turn to grab a handful.

If by chance the number of beans you pick up is, say, seventeen, then you miss a turn. Why? Because seventeen is a prime number, and you would always have one bean left over, which the rules don't allow!

Solo Snap

Can you find a match before getting to the end of the pack?

You will need: A pack of playing cards.

Helps with: Counting concentration, and developing a sense of 'chance'.

This is a simple game of solitaire to teach your child.

Shuffle the pack and start with the cards face down in a pile, then have your child turn them over one at a time.

Now as your child turns the cards over, they say, in order, 'ace, two, three . . .' and so on up to 'Ten, Jack, Queen, King', then start again at 'Ace, two . . .' If they turn over a card that is the same as the one they have just said, that's a snap.

If they get a snap before reaching the end of the pack, they earn a point; if they don't get a snap they lose one point.

They start on five points and the aim is to get to ten points (they lose if they drop to zero points).

Sometimes the whole pack can be dealt without a single snap. But this happens only about a third of the time, so your child should end up winning more often than they lose.

Replica!

Give instructions to recreate a picture

You will need: Paper and a pencil.

Helps with: Language of mathematical description.

This game for two players is a great challenge to try when you have a bit of time to kill with your child – in a waiting room, at home around the table while the pasta cooks, waiting to be served at a restaurant.

Secretly draw a picture of a person or an animal; your picture must be entirely made up of triangles, circles, squares and rectangles. For example, the eyes might be triangles, the legs might be thin rectangles. Whoever draws first describes to the other player what they have drawn and he or she then has to try and replicate the structure.

The instruction might start: 'Draw a rectangle about five centimetres long and two centimetres high.' Or, using hands to indicate: 'Draw a rectangle about this big.'

Whoever is trying to recreate the picture can ask questions to find out more.

Reveal your picture and see how close the duplicate is.

Bull's Eye

Turn mental arithmetic into a game of archery

You will need: Paper and a pencil.

Helps with: Mental arithmetic, from basic addition to any more advanced calculations that your child can handle, such as squares, fractions or negative numbers.

Think of a secret number (which we will call the Target) and scribble it down on your bit of paper. Then set a series of instructions that, if followed correctly, end up at the target number. When your child gets the answer you've written down, reveal it and say, 'Bull's eye.'

Let's say your Target is six. You can now set a series of instructions, which you can either make up as you go along, or (if you find mental arithmetic tricky yourself) you can prepare earlier.

For example you could say, 'Start with the number two... Double it... Add seven... Take away one... Halve that number... Add three... Take away two... And where has your imaginary arrow landed?'

With any luck, it has landed on six, at which point you reveal the piece of paper as you say, 'Bull's eye.'

You can of course make the instructions as easy or as hard as you want, but you do want your child to get Bull's eye most (if not all) of the time, so set the level appropriately.

The game can also be reversed — your child can set you a target and then create the instructions.

86

Egg-Timer Challenge

Challenge your child to beat their own record

You will need: A photocpy of the grid overleaf and a timer – a three-minute egg timer is ideal but the timer on your phone is also fine.

Helps with: Learning times tables.

In the same way that athletes train to beat a personal best on the track, challenge your child to beat their personal best in times tables.

Choose which table they are going to work on. They have exactly three minutes to multiply as many of the forty-eight numbers in the grid by the tables number (say, multiplying each number by three). They write the answers in the space alongside each number. Start the timer...

This activity becomes much more exciting if it is a challenge to beat a previous record. How many can they get right in three minutes? Is that better than they did last time? Use a timer with seconds to record how quickly they can do all the calculations. And do keep a note somewhere of their personal best. It might be days or weeks before they beat it.

1 x	4 x	3 x	2 x
8 x	11 x	7 x	12 x
4 x	7 x	10 x	3 x
10 x	1 x	9 x	8 x
5 x	2 x	12 x	6 x
7 x	8 x	3 x	5 x
6 x	9 x	5 x	10 x
2 x	4 x	1 x	6 x
5 x	9 x	11 x	1 x
11 x	12 x	2 x	4 x
7 x	8 x	10 x	3 x
12 x	9 x	11 x	6 x

Out and About

Maths can crop up in the unlikeliest of places, like hubcaps and seesaws. Encourage your child to keep their mathematical eyes open, whether it's in the garden, walking down the street or out in the park.

Hubcap and Manhole Geekery

Turn the most boring of everyday objects into an intriguing discovery

Helps with: Spotting mathematical patterns.

Do you ever look at the hubcaps on cars? Or at manhole covers? Of course not – only the saddest of geeks would be interested in something like that. Yet that is exactly what we're going to recommend that you do. Because hubcaps and manhole covers are just two examples of everyday objects that can feature surprisingly interesting patterns.

As you walk along the street, what's the first car you can see? What does the hubcap look like? How many spokes are there? Five or six maybe? The spokes probably form a rather elegant star. Or perhaps it doesn't have spokes; it might have holes instead. How many are there? Eight? What's that shape called?

Manhole covers often have an array of bumps and other intricate shapes that must be there for some reason. Are they somebody's code for something? Are they all the same?

Incidentally, it can be better for manhole covers to be round rather than square. Making them round means that you can put the cover back without worrying about getting the angle right. And because a circle has a constant diameter, there's no risk of the manhole cover falling down the hole if you replace it 'the wrong way', whereas it is possible to drop a square manhole cover into its hole, by turning it on its edge and placing it across the diagonal.

88

Shortcut

Can you shorten your walking distance?

Helps with: Estimation, measurement and triangles.

If there's somewhere that you and your child walk to frequently – to school, or to the shops perhaps – you can investigate which route is shortest. This is particularly good if the way to get there involves crossing a grid of streets. Is it quicker for your route to be a giant 'L' shape, or do you save distance if you do it as a series of left-right turns that zigzag you through the roads?

The only way to find out for sure is to measure it. You can do this by counting paces, but be sure that you use the same length of step all the time. Or, if you have a pedometer, that can do the work for you (there are apps you can download for this, if you trust their accuracy).

On quiet roads, you can experiment with saving distance by crossing diagonally. How much distance do you save if you take the dotted line route in the diagram?

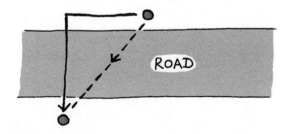

Once you've established that diagonals do save you distance, you can even investigate which diagonal saves you the *most* distance. (To save you having to work it out, the best shortcut is to cross roads, parks and fields at an angle of 45 degrees. This reduces the distance you walk by a whopping 30 per cent.)

Your child may not appreciate it yet, but this is a gentle introduction to the world of right-angled triangles and Pythagoras, something they'll be seeing plenty of when they are older.

How Many Bounces?

Investigate the properties of a dropped ball

Helps with: Time, reasoning and predicting.

If you have a ball with you in the park, you can investigate its bouncing. Drop the ball and together count how many times it bounces before it stops.

There are lots of different questions your child can try to answer:

- Can they make it bounce more times?

- What effect does throwing it higher have?

- Or using more force to bounce it?

- If you have two different balls, which one stops bouncing first?

- To count as a 'bounce', does there have to be a gap between the ball and the ground?

Most curious of all, what happens to the time between bounces? You'll notice it gets shorter and shorter. Maybe the ball bounces faster and faster until in the end it is bouncing infinitely fast . . . at which point it has stopped.

Discovering Parabolas

Watch the path of a ball in the air

Helps with: Learning about curves.

When playing catch or kicking a football with your child, get them to look at the path that the ball takes through the air. Does it travel in a straight line? They'll probably spot that it actually travels in a curve, but what is that curve?

The curved shape that children are most familiar with is a circle. 'Maybe a ball going through the air is making part of a circle,' you can suggest. But (with a bit of prompting) you can realise together that if it's a circle then after a while the ball should start looping back towards the thrower. That doesn't happen, does it? ('That's because the ground gets in the way,' said one child when confronted with this question.)

You can both try to draw the path with your finger, or with a pencil on a piece of paper.

Back at home, a fun (if slightly messy) way to discover the shape of a ball flying through the air is with a marble and some paint. Put a big piece of paper on the table, and tilt the table by sticking books under two of the legs. Now dip the marble in the paint, and gently roll it up the slope of the paper, at an angle, then let it roll back down. The path of the marble will be marked out by a line of paint.

If you want a less messy version, there are apps for your phone that will track the path of a moving object, an effect that is known as 'Stromotion'.

The shape is known a parabola, and you don't need a ball to produce it. Next time you're heading out on a long journey, you might suggest (if you have boys!): 'OK, before we go, has everyone done a parabola?'

91

Seesaw Balance

Discover Archimedes' lever principle in the playground

Helps with: Doubling, halving and the principle of levers and balancing.

Seesaws are great when two friends get on, but when it's an adult and child at either end it's less fun. The child is left dangling in the air while the adult plummets to the ground.

This is, however, a chance to experiment with balancing. One way to do it is to find a second child in the playground to share the seat at one end. Two children may not exactly balance an adult, but it'll be close enough to be able to propel yourselves up and down. And you have a nice equation: one adult equals two children.

If there aren't any spare children around, the way to balance the seesaw is for the adult to move towards the centre (or fulcrum) of the seesaw and perch on the bar. It's not very comfortable, but there will be a point at which adult and child perfectly balance.

This is a beautiful demonstration of the lever principle, first explained by Archimedes over two thousand years ago. If you have two objects, one of them twice the weight of the other, then for the two to balance, the lighter object (the child in this case) needs to be twice as far from the fulcrum as the heavier one (you).

92

Which Way is North?

Work out which direction you are going without needing a compass

Helps with: Angles and direction.

Wherever you are outdoors, there are clues that will help you work out which direction you are heading. During the day, the most useful guide of all is the sun. At the start of the day it will be in the east, at lunchtime (in the northern hemisphere) it is roughly south (or north if you are in the southern hemisphere), and at the end of the day it's in the west. There are ways of working the direction out much more accurately using the hands of a watch as a compass, but to be honest a rough check based on the position of the sun and time of day is usually enough.

This is a great collaborative exercise with your child. First you need to find the sun (a bit tricky on cloudy days, but you can usually tell roughly where it is). Then check the time. If it's ten o'clock in the morning in the UK, then the sun is somewhere between east and south – in other words, it's roughly south-east. Now, together, you can act like a compass. 'If we're pointing to the sun then that is south-east ... so behind us will be ... north-west. South is just a bit to the right of the sun, and west is a quarter turn to the right from south.'

In built-up areas there are other clues. Most satellite dishes (in the UK) point south-east (they are pointing to the main geo-stationary satellite, and that's where it happens to be). Older churches almost always point east–west, with the main entrance at the west end and the tower or spire (above the altar) at the east end. And if you can't see a church, maybe you can find a cricket pitch. They usually face north–south for a simple reason: the batsmen don't want to be facing directly into the sun at the end of the day.

.

How High is That?

Work out the height of trees and buildings using a crisp packet

Helps with: Problem solving, geometry and measuring.

If you are out in the park, there's a really simple way to estimate the height of a tree. And all you need is a crisp packet – or something else that's rectangular and can be folded (an envelope, a scrap of paper).

First, fold down the corner of the crisp packet so that the corner is on the other side of the packet and the edges line up, like this:

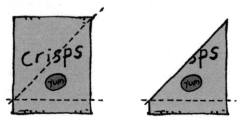

Make a crease along the diagonal – which is half a right angle, or 45 degrees.

The next part needs two of you. One of you holds the packet up to your eye, so you are looking up the diagonal as if it is the sight of a gun. The other has to make sure that the bottom of the crisp packet is horizontal, rather than being tilted up or down.

Now, whichever of you is holding the crisp packet should walk forwards until the top of the tree is lined up with your sight along the crisp packet.

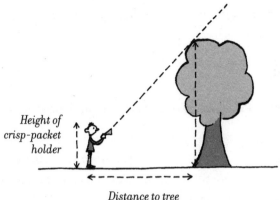

Height of crisp-packet holder

Distance to tree

When the top of the tree lines up, the crisp-packet holder stands still while the other counts how many paces it is from there to the trunk of the tree. And that – plus the height of the person holding the crisp-packet – is the same as the height of the tree.

You can measure the height of lamp posts, towers, anything you want. Just make sure you – and the thing you are measuring – aren't on a hill.

How Far is That Chimney?

Discover how 'parallax' can tell you how far away something is

Helps with: Estimation, and a way of using similar triangles.

Stretch out your arm, close one eye and hold up a finger so that it blocks out something you can see in the distance – a chimney on a house, say. Now open that eye and close the other one. Your finger will appear to jump to the side, away from the chimney! This curious phenomenon is known as parallax.

You and your child can use it to make a very rough estimate of how far away a chimney on a roof is. When your finger jumps to the side, try and work out how far along the roof of the house it jumps. The rule of thumb (or maybe that should be 'rule of finger') is that the distance to the chimney is about ten times* the distance by which your finger jumps. If your finger jumps by the full width of the house roof, this means that the chimney is about ten house-roof-widths away from you.

---

* This technique is to do with similar triangles. For most people, the distance from their eyes to an outstretched finger is about ten times the distance between their eyes. This ratio of 10:1 is the same as the ratio of the distance that the chimney moves to the distance from the chimney to your finger.

A typical terraced house is about five metres wide, so if your finger jumps by the width of a terraced house, the chimney is very roughly $5 \times 10 = 50$ metres away.

If you want to get really ambitious, you can use this method to try and work out the distance to the moon. Estimate how many moon-widths your finger jumps when you switch eyes. The moon is about 2,000 miles across, so if your finger jumps by twelve moon-widths, that would mean the moon is about 2,000 miles $\times$ 12 finger jumps $\times$ 10, which is 240,000 miles. (Now check what the actual distance is . . .)

Maths Magic

While some people think that the whole of
mathematics is magic – a complete mystery –
simple numerical magic tricks not only provide
a fun context for some mental arithmetic, they
also tap into kids' pleasure at learning tricks.

95

Thought Control

Turn mental arithmetic into a bit of magic

Helps with: Mental arithmetic.

Try this trick on your child. Don't rush them!

'Think of a number, any number, but keep it secret... OK, now double your number... Next add six to that answer... Divide your new number by two (so find half of that number)... Finally take away the number you started with.

'Oh, I'm getting a vision... I can see a number looming in front of my eyes... Have you finished on the number [drum roll]... three?'

With a bit of luck, they *have* ended on three, and will be suitably amazed. If they haven't ended on three, check what their starting number was. Suppose it was four. Say, 'Oh, maybe it doesn't work with even numbers. Let's just check.' Then go through the steps again: 'Four... Double it makes eight... Add six makes fourteen... Half of that is seven... Seven take away the number you started with (four) makes – oh, it DOES make three. Wow.'

You can then check out this trick for any numbers you like, and sure enough, no matter how complicated the number is (some children think they'll catch the trick out with fractions or negative numbers) it will always end at three.

Once your child has mastered the rules, encourage them to try the trick out on a tame relative who is good at playing along. Children love the power of being able to mind-read what Grandma finished on.

Zoo Prediction

Another mathematical mind-reading trick

Helps with: Mental arithmetic.

Think of a number between one and ten. Multiply it by nine. If your answer has two digits, add those two digits together (so if it's twenty-seven you would add 2 + 7).

Take away four from your answer.

Turn the number you now have into a letter, using the formula one is A, two is B, three is C... and so on.

Think of an animal beginning with your letter, and close your eyes and have a picture of your animal in your head. Is it big, and grey, with a trunk, by any chance?

How does this work? Whatever the number you choose to multiply by nine, the digits of the answer will also always add up to nine. So: 4 × 9 = 36, 3 + 6 = 9. Or 8 × 9 = 72, 7 + 2 = 9. This is a curious property of the nine times table. For numbers larger than ten the digits don't always add up to nine, but they will add to a multiple of nine. In fact, if you keep adding the digits they will eventually add up to 9... So 21 × 9 = 189, and 1 + 8 + 9 = 18, and 1 + 8 = 9.

Age Magic

Multiply your child's age by the five magic numbers

You will need: A calculator.

Helps with: Multiplication, factors.

This trick works with children aged nine or under.

'This calculator loves children your age. I'll show you.' Enter your child's age on the calculator – let's suppose they are eight.

Now tell them there are five magic numbers – 3, 7, 11, 13 and 37 – and they all combine to make a potion.

> 'Which number do you want first?'

> 'Thirteen.'

Multiply their age (eight) by thirteen on the calculator (but instead of saying 'Multiplied by thirteen', say 'Abracadabra thirteen').

> You: 'Next number?'

> Child: 'Three.'

> You: 'Abracadabra three. Next?'

> Child: 'Thirty-seven.'

> You: 'Abracadabra thirty-seven. Next?'

And so on. After entering the fifth and final magic number, say 'Alla-kazam' and press equals. Their age will appear across the screen six times, 888 888.

(If your child is ten or older, they'll still like the effect — it's just you can't do it with their age. Simply ask them to pick a number between one and nine.)

98

The Twisted Loop

A curious case of one plus one equals one

You will need: Scissors, paper and sticky tape.

Helps with: Thinking about shapes and edges.

Cut (or carefully tear) a strip from a sheet of paper. It's best if it's about 4cm wide. If you want, draw a dotted line along the centre of the strip, so it looks like a road. Now join the ends of the strip together to make a loop, but before you tape them, give one end a half-twist, as shown in the diagram. You are now ready to perform the 'trick'.

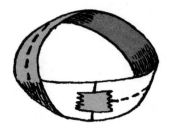

Carefully cut along the dotted line. 'I'm cutting this in half,' you say, 'and when you cut things in half how many pieces do you get?' 'Two,' comes the reply. 'Not if it's magic,' you say, and sure enough as you make the final snip the single loop turns into... a bigger single loop.

This mysterious twisted loop is called a Mobius Strip. You can discover other interesting things about it. Imagine you are an ant, with very muddy feet. Get the ant (your fingers) to walk along the middle of the band (along the dotted line, if you drew one) leaving his muddy footprints – use a pen to mark the prints. The ant keeps going until . . . he gets back to the start. Now here's a strange thing: his footprints are over the entire strip, even though he never went over the edge. In other words, a Mobius Strip is a shape with only one 'side'. If you run your finger along the edge you'll discover that the loop only has one edge, too.

If that isn't enough excitement, see what happens if you give the strip of paper a full twist before sticking the ends together, and then cut along the middle as before.

Yet stranger things happen if you make a half-twist and start cutting one third of the way in from the edge.

Stacking Dice

Add invisible numbers

You will need: at least three dice.

Helps with: Arithmetic, especially the seven times table.

Your child adds the invisible numbers on the top and bottom of the dice

$$6+2+1+5+2 = \underline{\underline{16}}$$

This is an easy trick for your child to learn, and when they start to perform it they will be practising the seven-times table and some subtraction.

Demonstrate it like this. First, ask them to put three dice into a stack while your back is turned.

You now turn around. 'There are five faces on the dice that I can't see,' you declare, 'but I'm going to use the power of X-ray vision to add them up.' You write down the total on a piece of paper and fold it to keep your prediction a secret.

Now, together, you add up the five hidden faces. Let's say they are $6 + 2 + 5 + 1 + 2 = 16$. You slowly unfurl the piece of paper to reveal your prediction, which is . . . Sixteen!

How does it work? The numbers on the opposite sides of a dice always add to seven. This means that the top and bottom numbers on the three stacked dice will add to $3 \times 7 = 21$. All you have to do is subtract from 21 the number you can see on the top of the stack. If the number on the top of the stack is five, your prediction is $21 - 5 = 16$.

You can do this with as many dice as you want. With six dice, for example, just multiply six by seven to get to forty-two. Then subtract from that the number on the top of the stack and write down your prediction.

100

Mirror Magic

Words that miraculously stay the same in the mirror

Helps with: Shape recognition and symmetry.

Turn this page upside down and look at it in the mirror. The word 'QUALITY' will be completely messed up, yet as if by magic, the word 'CHOICE' remains exactly the same.

CHOICE

QUALITY

Why is this?

How many other words can your child find that don't get ruined when viewed upside down in the mirror? What's the longest word they can find that has this magic quality? (The longest we've found is 'KICKBOXED' – as long as you agree that's a real word.)

101

Reverse and Add

You predict what your child's numbers will add to

You will need: Paper and a pencil.

Helps with: Arithmetic, pattern spotting.

Ask your child to think of a two-digit number and secretly write it down. Suppose they have thought of 49. Now get them to tell you what the two digits of their number add up to (in this case the digits are 4 and 9, so they tell you the sum, which is 13). Whatever they tell you, secretly multiply that number by 11 (see the shortcut to doing this on page 69) and write the answer down as your prediction (143 in this case). Fold it up and put it to one side.

Ask your child to reverse their two-digit number (so 49 reverses to 94) and now get them to add those two numbers together – you can help them, since your prediction is already written down: 49 plus 94 is 143.

Reveal your prediction, and take the applause.

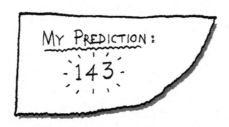

Index by maths topic

This index is a quick guide to finding a game or activity by maths topic. However, many of the activities in the book can be used to bring up any part of maths that you want to work on with your child — from counting to geometry and general problem solving.

Acknowledgements

Our thanks go to: Andrew Jeffrey, Rob Elias, Cath Frances, Alison Young, Ed Faulkner, Mary Chamberlain, Eugenie Todd, Tom Hancock, Rachel O'Riordan, James Gooding, Becky Lovelock, Hugh Hunt, Elaine Standish and Pete Sanders.

And to Jenna, Adam and Josie for being such willing guinea pigs.